LOVE/SICK

BY JOHN CARIANI

2023 EDITION

LOVE/SICK

Copyright © 2016, 2018, 2023, John Cariani

All Rights Reserved

MUSIC AND THIRD-PARTY MATERIALS USE NOTE

IMPORTANT BILLING AND CREDIT REQUIREMENTS

ACKNOWLEDGMENTS

It takes so many people to make a play. What follows is a list of good, smart, kind people who helped me make LOVE/SICK. (Omissions and errors—while inexcusable—are inadvertent.)

For helping me bring LOVE/SICK into the world, I wish to—wholeheartedly—thank…

…Ibi Janko, Wendy Stetson, Chris Brandjes, Angi Parks, Nicole Alifante, Mike Borrelli, Elizabeth Nicholas Synnott, Chris Edwards, Jack Cummings III, Barbara Walsh, Susan Lovell, Mari Okuda, Stephanie Klapper, Dee Ann Newkirk, Marla Ratner, Steve Campo, Rob Ruggiero, David Zarko, and Jack Thomas, for all they did before ALMOST, MAINE and LOVE/SICK became plays.

…Chris Campbell and everyone at the Barrow Group, for helping these plays find their way into the world, and Julie and Dave Walsh and John Lloyd, for running through the streets of New York City to see one of those early Barrow Group presentations.

…Kit Rodgers, Austin Fishbaugh, Courtney Janvrin, Sam Lloyd, Lexie McDonough, Trisha Mills, Carolyn Moe, David Sheehy, Joey Sousa, Mike Morris, Sara Shwab, and everyone at the International Thespian Society, Eastern Region, at Winnacunnett High School in Hampton, NH, for introducing LOVE/SICK to high school students.

…Jack Heifner, Connie Congdon, Scott Shattuck, Juanita Finkenberg, Jackie Rosenfeld, Benny May, Meaghan Cybulski, Jennifer Simms, Stephen Graham, Lamar Jefferson, Nick Pinelli, Jennifer Suter, Samantha Walker, Erin Whitmire, and everyone at the Festival of New American Plays at Stephen F. Austin State University, for the developmental reading.

…David Ledingham, Donald Sage Mackay, Louis Lotorto, Lyn Aliya, Janice Estey, Obadiah Jones, Zoe Levine, Mike Monroney, Lee Sullivan, Mark Thomas, Jeannie Walla, and everyone at the

Festival of New American Plays at the Aspen Fringe Festival, for the developmental reading.

…Dan Burson, Ben Ferber, Rob Cameron, Abbie Killeen, Dustin Tucker, Tess Van Horn, Todd Backus, Emily Mahaffey, Shannon Stockwell, Ella Wrenn, and everyone at Portland Stage Company's Little Festival of the Unexpected, for the workshop and staged reading.

…Dan Burson, Peter Brown, Matt Delameter, Janice O'Rourke, and Bess Weldon, for the other unexpected reading.

…Michael Rhodes, Paul Nugent, Anna Nugent, Andrea Rhodes, Brendan Burke, Larry Lowry, Amy Olson, Jen Skura, Jill Van Note, Steven Austin Young, and everyone at Tangent Theater Company and AboutFACE Ireland, for the NEWvember Festival reading.

…Matt Graber, Sarah Bauer, Noelle Toland, Danielle Doucette, Andy Hyman, Angela Oh, Kristin Lee Kelly, Jason Weiss, Justin Alston, and everyone at the Blank Theatre's Living Room Series, for the staged reading.

…Jim Fagan, Patrick Lynch, Zachary Booth, Pat Buckley, Eddie Carnevale, Carolyn Charpie, Valorie Curry, Elizabeth Davis, Adriana DeGirolami, Jerzy Gwiazdowski, Justin Hagan, Jenny Kirlin, Seth Kirschner, Kate White Morris, Jennifer Mudge, Anthony Rapp, Sara Thigpen, Sam Underwood, Brian Williams, Katy Wright-Mead, Alex Wyse, Malorie Bryant, Evan Powell, and everyone involved in the Hemophilia Association of New York benefit.

…Andy Polk, Dan Winerman, Stacy Lynn Gould, Christina Barrell, Reuben Barsky, Hugh Buller, Eloise Edwards, Txai Frota, Alia Guitry, James Lindsay, Penny O'Brien, Alex Pepperman, Nikki Pope, Gerome Samonte, and everyone involved in the workshop at the American Academy of Dramatic Arts.

…Joe Cacaci, Jim Frangione, Bob Jaffe, Matthew Penn, Lori Bashour, Valerie Bjur Carlson, Dan Winerman, Farah Alvin,

Jeff Biehl, Cindy Cheung, Tor Hillhouse, Evelyn Dumont, PJ Grisar, Elise Lockwood, and everyone at the Berkshire Playwrights Lab, for the staged reading.

…Skip Greer, Jenni Werner, Becca Poccia, Jenny Daniels, Mark Cuddy, Donnetta Lavinia Grays, Dave Mason, Kathy McCafferty, Ron Menzel, Meg Richardson, and everyone at Geva, for the staged reading.

…Lisa Klages, Brandon Bacorn, Brittany Bonnell, Alexis Gedallovich, Matt Heston, Jenna Kate Karn, Elyssa Kohen, Emma Mohrmann, Anthony Papastrat, Zoe Benditt, Sadie Alisa, Jessica Pizzuti, Morgan Taylor, Evan Hawkins, Emily King, Maddie Suvurunsgi, Cory Raynor, Shannen Adamites, Julianne Boyd, Stephanie Yankwitt, Corinne Miller, Jeff Roudabush, and everyone at Barrington Stage Company, for the "Cariani Evening."

…Gerry Roe, Sarah Brewer, Bridget Baugh, Chris Carapucci, Broderick Cornett, Paulina DeGraff Hansen, Alan Eliston, Tessa Fraser, Joe Garcia, Andrew Heaton, Jack Jennaway, Jeff Kuykendall, Sian Laine, Lynn Laubach, Richard Leeds, Taylor Leidheisel, Kassidy Miller, Carl Redman, Dodie Rife, Teresa Sarkela, Gwendolyn Satterfield, Miranda Wallace, Ryan Wallace, Kaitlyn Welsh, and everyone at Rocky Mountain College, for the developmental production.

…Katy Wright-Mead, Liza Fernandez, Ryman Sneed, Caroline Kinsolving, Joel Ganz, Don Guillory, Kathleen Chalfant, Blair Baker, Justin Hagan, Tor Hillhouse, Chris Thorn, Dave Mason, and Pascale Armand, for the Royal Family Productions readings.

…William Allison, Todd Backus, Skye Barkley, Lila Becker, Courtney Bedgood, Jordan Bennett-Barnes, Anna Bernard, Christina Bracken, Brandon Browning, Elizabeth Burroughs, Rochelle Cady, Chris Carter, Michael Castillo, Cecelia Chapman, Molly Chiffer, Blair Cooper, Joe Court, Alanea Cremen, Evan Cullinan, Bryelle Dafeldecker, Bianca Di Carlo, Becca Donald, Nikki Eak, Megan Eckert, Courtney Feiman, Max Flicker, Ashley Flowers, Caitlighn Foley, Ted Gallant, Savada Gilmore, Jared Goldenberg, Lindsay Green,

Andrew Harris, Megan Harris, Colin Hart, Ryan Hemsoth, Lauren Henkel, Russell Hill, Chris Hourcle, DeAnna Hughes, Dan Im, Sharjeel Khan, Hyun Sook Kim, Charlotte Knapp, Neal Knapp, Dave Leach, Crystal Liu, Savannah Lobel, Greg Lund, Cait Malloy, Brandon Malott, Mickie Marie, Joe Marra, Caitlin Margolien, Alex Mathis, Jamison Meyer, David Mikulay, Turner Morehead, Jessica Morrison, Melanie Mortimore, Kimmie Naus, Sven Henry Nelson, Michael O'Hara, Moira O'Sullivan, Eric Ort, Megan Otteson, Sydney Peterson, Lauren Pivirotto, Rachel Rogers, Kat Rother, LeAnna Rothwell, Carl Rugato, John Sadler, Megan Santiago, Caroline Scherer, Michael Schmalz, Jackie Seijo, Kip Shawger, Zach Shore, Kyle Stoffers, Melanie Thomas, Zoe Turi, Andrea VanSwearingen, Alicia Whavers, Graham Zellers, and Courtney Ziegler, for lending their expertise and/or time, whether they wanted to or not.

…Erich Dicenzo and the Fairfax High School cast and crew, for helping me believe that high school students can do this play.

…Leah Dach, Abigail Barker, Keira Bug-Wiltse, Amaya Johnson, Matthew Brauhn, Tristin C., Eliana Caprye, Claire Duggan, Alex Dokken, Blythe Fain, Michael Fornter, Ember Havner, Rey Hertel, Johann Kohls, Autumn Morris, Eden O'Neill, Kaydence Robinette, Garret S., Kennedy Scott, Ryann Valley, and Brenna White of North Central High School in Spokane, Washington, for helping me as I reworked Scene 8, "Sick of This," for this, the 2023 edition of LOVE/SICK.

…Kathy Hogg and Aislinn Frantz, for proofreading.

And special thanks to the dramaturgs or people who acted like dramaturgs: Nicole Alifante, Jazzmin Bonner, Dan Burson, Jack Cummings III, Chris Edwards, Ben Ferber, Aislinn Frantz, Kaci Goodworth, Andy Hyman, Benny May, Miles Orduna, Eric Ort, Becca Poccia, Andrea Redmount, Amy Saltz, Jenni Werner, and Sally Wood. Making plays is impossible without the likes of you.

Extra special thanks to Jay Putnam. You loom large and save scenes. And you made this play with me.

Extra, extra special thanks to Betsy Hogg and Aislinn Frantz, for helping to create this edition.

Extra, extra, extra special thanks to my family: to Paul and Sheila and Jeff and Henry and Isaac Cariani, for always making me feel loved; and to John Lloyd, for helping me understand love and sickness, and that you can't have one without the other.

LOVE/SICK received its world premiere production at Portland Stage Company (Anita Stewart, Artistic Director; Cami Barrantes, Managing Director) in Portland, Maine, opening on March 29, 2013. It was directed by Sally Wood, the set design was by Anita Stewart, the costume design was by Kathleen Brown, the lighting design was by Bryon Winn, the sound design was by Chris Fitze, the incidental music was by Julian Fleisher, the production stage manager was Shane Van Vleit. The play was comprised of ten short plays, and the cast was as follows:

OBSESSIVE IMPULSIVE .... Abigail Killeen, David Mason
THE SINGING TELEGRAM .... Torsten Hillhouse,
Patricia Buckley
WHAT?!? .... David Mason, Torsten Hillhouse
THE ANSWER .... Abigail Killeen, Torsten Hillhouse
UH-OH .... David Mason, Patricia Buckley
LUNCH AND DINNER .... Abigail Killeen, Torsten Hillhouse
CHICKEN .... Abigail Killeen, David Mason
WHERE WAS I? .... Abigail Killeen, Patricia Buckley
FORGOT .... David Mason, Patricia Buckley
DESTINY .... Patricia Buckley, Torsten Hillhouse

LOVE/SICK had its first developmental production at High Point University (Ed Simpson, Chair) in High Point, North Carolina, opening on September 30, 2010. It was directed by Jay Putnam, the set and lighting designs were by Matthew Emerson, the costume design was by Ami Shupe, the sound design was by Daniel Horney, the production stage manager was Amanda Mayes. The play was comprised of eight short plays, and the cast was as follows:

OBSESSIVE IMPULSIVE .... Anna-Parsons Charles,
Dan Moldovan
THE SINGING TELEGRAM .... Maggie Jo Saylor, Daniel Harr
THE ANSWER .... Marie Ventrone, Nathan Ruffin
UH-OH .... Jennifer Arnold, Cody Russell
LUNCH AND DINNER .... Cate Lightburn, Nathan Ruffin
CHICKEN .... Maggie Jo Saylor, Cody Russell

FORGOT .... Marie Ventrone, Daniel Harr
DESTINY .... Anna-Parsons Charles, Dan Moldovan

LOVE/SICK had its second developmental production at Ball State University (William Jenkins, Chair) in Muncie, Indiana, opening on November 1, 2012. It was directed by Eva Patton, the set design was by Bri Kuffell, the costume design was by Tyler Phillips, the lighting design was by Adam Kelly, the sound design was by Bryan Martina, the production stage manager was Caitie Noller. The play was comprised of ten short plays, and the cast was as follows:

OBSESSIVE IMPULSIVE .... Cole Abell, Nancy Hale
THE SINGING TELEGRAM .... Katie Stofko, Edric Mitchell
WHAT?!? .... Jon Whitney, Brad Root
THE ANSWER .... Bradford Reilly, Kara Schoenhofer
UH-OH .... Amber Price, Jack McFarlane
LUNCH AND DINNER .... Macie Tonn, Jon Whitney
CHICKEN .... Brad Root, Cynthia Nesbit
WHERE WAS I? .... Sarah Paradise, Kara Schoenhofer
FORGOT .... Cole Abell, Katie Stofko
DESTINY .... Bradford Reilly, Macie Tonn

LOVE/SICK received a professional developmental production at Shadowland Theatre (Brendan Burke, Artistic Director) in Ellenville, New York, opening on June 21, 2013. It was directed by John Cariani and Brendan Burke, the set design was by Drew Francis, the costume design was by Holly Budd, the lighting design was by Chris Hallenbeck, the sound design was by Jeff Knapp, the incidental music was by Julian Fleisher, the production stage manager was Brittney Green. The play was comprised of ten short plays, and the cast was as follows:

OBSESSIVE IMPULSIVE .... Katie Hartke, David Mason
THE SINGING TELEGRAM .... Daniel Robert Sullivan,
                                                                      Kathy McCafferty
WHAT?!? .... Daniel Robert Sullivan, David Mason
THE ANSWER .... Katie Hartke, Daniel Robert Sullivan

UH-OH .... Kathy McCafferty, David Mason
LUNCH AND DINNER .... Daniel Robert Sullivan,
Katie Hartke
CHICKEN .... Katie Hartke, David Mason
FORGOT .... David Mason, Kathy McCafferty
WHERE WAS I? .... Katie Hartke, Kathy McCafferty
DESTINY .... Kathy McCafferty, Daniel Robert Sullivan

LOVE/SICK received a professional developmental production at
the Public Theatre (Christopher Schario, Executive/Artistic Director;
Janet Mitchko, Co-Artistic Director) in Lewiston, Maine, opening
on October 1, 2013. It was directed by Christopher Schario, the set
design was by Dan Bilodeau, the costume design was by Hannah J.
Brown, the lighting design was by Bart Garvey, the sound design was
by Larry French, the production stage manager was Lisa Bragdon. The
play was comprised of ten short plays, and the cast was as follows:

OBSESSIVE IMPULSIVE .... William Peden, Heather Dilly
THE SINGING TELEGRAM .... Sarah Corey, Torsten Hillhouse
WHAT?!? .... William Peden, Torsten Hillhouse
THE ANSWER .... Heather Dilly, William Peden
UH-OH .... Sarah Corey, Torsten Hillhouse
LUNCH AND DINNER .... Heather Dilly, Torsten Hillhouse
CHICKEN .... Sarah Corey, William Peden
WHERE WAS I? .... Heather Dilly, Sara Corey
FORGOT .... William Peden, Heather Dilly
DESTINY .... Sarah Corey, Torsten Hillhouse

LOVE/SICK received a professional developmental production at
Half Moon Theatre Company (Molly Katz, Executive Director;
Kristy Grimes, Managing Director; Patty Wineapple, Producer) in
Poughkeepsie, New York, opening on November 1, 2013. It was
directed by Christopher V. Edwards, the set design and props were
by Aaron Ethan Green, the costume design was by Charlotte Palmer,
the lighting design was by Jared H. Goldstein, the sound design was
by Jeff Knapp, the production stage manager was Michael Castillo.

The play was comprised of ten short plays, and the cast was as follows:

OBSESSIVE IMPULSIVE .... Jennifer Skura, Jack Corcoran
THE SINGING TELEGRAM .... Jack Corcoran, Shona Tucker
WHAT?!? .... Jack Corcoran, Greg Skura
THE ANSWER .... Jennifer Skura, Greg Skura
UH-OH .... Amy Lemon, Steven Patterson
LUNCH AND DINNER .... Jennifer Skura, Jack Corcoran
CHICKEN .... Shona Tucker, Greg Skura
WHERE WAS I? .... Amy Lemon, Shona Tucker
FORGOT .... Steven Patterson, Amy Lemon
DESTINY .... Shona Tucker, Steven Patterson

LOVE/SICK received a professional developmental production at TheaterWorks Hartford (Rob Ruggiero, Artistic Director; Nicole LaFlair Nieves, General Manager) in Hartford, Connecticut, opening on May 29, 2014. It was directed by Amy Saltz, the set design was by Michael Schweickhardt, the costume design was by Harry Nadal, the lighting design was by Mary Jo Dondlinger, the sound design was by Fitz Patton, the production stage manager was Kate Cudworth. The play was comprised of ten short plays, and the cast was as follows:

OBSESSIVE IMPULSIVE .... Laura Woodward, Bruch Reed
THE SINGING TELEGRAM .... Chris Thorn, Pascale Armand
WHAT?!? .... Chris Thorn, Bruch Reed
THE ANSWER .... Laura Woodward, Chris Thorn
UH-OH .... Pascale Armand, Bruch Reed
LUNCH AND DINNER .... Laura Woodward, Bruch Reed
CHICKEN .... Pascale Armand, Bruch Reed
FORGOT .... Chris Thorn, Laura Woodward
WHERE WAS I? .... Laura Woodward, Pascale Armand
DESTINY .... Laura Woodward, Chris Thorn

LOVE/SICK received a professional developmental production by Royal Family Productions (Christine Henry, Artistic Director) at the Royal Family Performing Arts Space (Evan Storey and Andy Theodorou, Producers) in New York City. It was directed by Christine Henry, the movement direction was by JoAnn M. Hunter, the set design was by Shannon Rednour, the costume design was by Lux Haac, the lighting design was by Lucrecia Briceno, the sound design was by Danny Erdberg, the incidental music was by Barton Kuebler, Lars Jacobsen, and Christine Henry, the production stage manager was Adrian Peña. The cast was as follows:

MAN, BEN, BILL, KEVIN .... Debargo Sanyal
WOMAN, CELIA, KELLY, JILL, LIZ, EMILY .... Dee Roscioli
SINGING TELEGRAM MAN,
ANDY, KEITH, MARK, JAKE .... Justin Hagan and John Cariani
LOUISE, SARAH, ABBIE .... Simone Harrison
SUPERCENTER DANCERS .... Jenn Aédo, Rachel Geisler,
Stephanie Israelson, Jolina Javier,
Schuyler Midgett

LOVE/SICK received a professional developmental production at Arc Stages (Adam David Cohen, Artistic Director; Marlene Canapi, Managing Director; Ann Shankman, President) in Pleasantville, New York, opening on September 25, 2015. It was directed by Stephanie Kovacs Cohen, the set design and props were by Ann Shankman, the costume design was by Libby Brennescholtz, the lighting design was by Adam Cohen, the sound design was by Stephanie Kovacs Cohen, the production stage manager was Emily C. Rolston. The cast was as follows:

MAN, ANDY, BILL, MARK .... Collin Smith
WOMAN, CELIA, KELLY, JILL, ABBIE .... Katie Hartke
SINGING TELEGRAM MAN,
BEN, KEITH, KEVIN, JAKE .... David Lanson
LOUISE, SARAH, LIZ, EMILY .... Caroline Kinsolving

THE PLAYS

LOVE/SICK is a one-act, nine- (or ten-) play cycle about love and loss—but mostly loss. Each play has its own arc and tells the story of a couple at a crossroads in their relationship. Since each relationship is more advanced than the previous relationship, a larger arc emerges, and the individual plays work together to create a satisfying whole—one that chronicles the life cycle of a typical relationship from meeting through divorce…and afterwards.

The plays:
1. "Obsessive Impulsive"
2. "The Singing Telegram"
3. "What?!?"
4. "The Answer"
5. "Uh-Oh"
6. "Lunch and Dinner"
[Bonus Scene: "Chicken"]
7. "Forgot"
8. "Sick of This"
9. "Destiny"

LOVE/SICK was originally published as a nine-play cycle, but can also be performed as a ten-play cycle. Please see the Bonus Scene on page 108 of this script for information.

LOVE/SICK works best as an intermission-less event. However, if the Bonus Scene is used and an intermission is desired, please take it after Scene 5, "Uh-Oh."

CHARACTERS

1. Obsessive Impulsive
A WOMAN and a MAN who fall in love at first sight.

2. The Singing Telegram
An inexperienced SINGING TELEGRAM MAN who delivers a life-changing singing telegram to an optimistic woman, LOUISE OVERBEE.

3. What?!?
BEN, a sweet guy who is surprised that he has fallen in love, and ANDY, the sweet guy he has fallen in love with.

4. The Answer
KEITH and CELIA, a groom and bride.

5. Uh-Oh
SARAH, a woman who wants to have some fun with her husband, BILL.

6. Lunch and Dinner
KELLY and MARK, a successful, seemingly happily married couple.

[Bonus Scene: Chicken
JASON, a man who has some doubts, and MADDIE, a woman who now also has some doubts.]

7. Forgot
JILL, a woman who wants more than she has, and KEVIN, her husband, who is happy with what he has.

8. Sick of This
ABBIE, a hard-working stay-at-home mom, and LIZ, her hard-working wife.

9. Destiny
JAKE, a recently divorced man, and EMILY, a recently divorced woman.

CHARACTER BREAKDOWN

LOVE/SICK is a play for four actors. With a cast of four, all actors should be in their 30s/early 40s.

LOVE/SICK can also be a play for eighteen actors and as many as twenty actors. (See the Bonus Scene on page 108 for more information.) Using a larger cast affords an opportunity to use actors of all ages. Since the characters in the earlier plays in LOVE/SICK are quite innocent, actors playing roles in the first few plays can be in their teens, 20s, and early 30s. Actors cast in the middle and later plays should be in their late 30s and older.

LOVE/SICK is meant to be performed by human beings, and human beings come in all kinds of shapes, sizes, genders, ethnicities, backgrounds, and abilities, so please cast accordingly.

Anyone who is comfortable playing the gender of the characters can play the roles.

TIME

7:30 P.M. on a Friday night in late September,
not too long ago—or maybe a long time ago.

PLACE

An alternate suburban reality.

NOTES FOR ACTORS, DIRECTORS, AND READERS

(If you are involved in a production of LOVE/SICK, please see the additional notes at the back of this volume.)

F. Scott Fitzgerald wrote, "The sentimental person thinks things will last—the romantic person has a desperate confidence that they won't."

I am a romantic. And so are the characters in LOVE/SICK. They are desperately confident that things are not going to last—and that things are going to go bad. But they fight like heck to make sure things last and don't go bad.

LOVE/SICK is a romantic play. It is not a sentimental play.

LOVE/SICK is full of highs and lows. Play them fully. Soar. Crash. Repeat.

LOVE/SICK is a realistically absurd play. Play it for real. Even though it's absurd.

LOVE/SICK is a very funny tragedy. Make sure it's very funny. And very sad.

Notes on Punctuation and Stage Directions:
LOVE/SICK employs a lot of very specific overlapping dialogue.

You'll often see this symbol: //. It will appear in the middle of lines or words, and it means that the next character to speak should begin their line where the // appears (and thereby interrupt the character who is currently speaking).

You'll also see this symbol: >. It means that the character who is speaking should keep talking and drive through to the end of their thought or point or sentence and not wait for the other character to speak.

Sometimes you'll see dialogue in brackets like these: [ ]. These words are not spoken. They're a guide to what a character leaves unsaid.

Sometimes you'll see commas after end punctuation. This is to encourage pace.

The stage direction *(Receives and processes.)* means just that. It's not a full beat—but a sorting through of what's going on or what's just been said.

Please don't completely dismiss the stage directions. Many are actions—actions that are as important as what is spoken.

LOVE/SICK

Scene 1: Obsessive Impulsive

It's 7:30 on a Friday night in late September in an alternate suburban reality.

Lights up on the SUPERCENTER. [The SuperCenter is like a Walmart or a Target or a Costco. Fun fact: Places like the SuperCenter or Walmart or Target or Costco are the places where people are likely to find love in over twenty states.]*

A MAN and a WOMAN push shopping carts through the SuperCenter. They are consulting shopping lists.

In a flash, the Man and the Woman catch sight of each other, GASP (because they take each other's breath away), rush to each other, and, from out of nowhere, KISS—a big, long (at least eight seconds), sloppy, passionate kiss.

They finally break, horrified by what they have just done.

[Note: When the Man and the Woman speak "in unison, to each other," it must be simultaneous and rapid-fire. Actors: In these unison sequences, you're speaking and listening and responding—all at the same time. Make sure that—while you speak—you are also listening and responding to each question/statement. You're taking in the same exact information you're providing—at the same exact time.]

MAN and WOMAN. *(In UNISON, to each other.)* Oh, my gosh!!! I am so sorry!—No, it's not you!—I know that's not an appropriate thing for a person to do, and I can totally explain why I just did that: You see, I'm obsessive impulsive, and—

* http://flowingdata.com/2013/02/22/map-of-craigslist-missed-connections/

> *Each quickly receives and processes what the other just said and then—incredulous and dumbfounded—asks:*

WHAT?!?

> *Each quickly receives and processes this question and then answers:*

I'm obsessive impulsive!

> *Each quickly receives and processes this extraordinary information—that someone else in the world might actually be obsessive impulsive!—and then, incredulous and dumbfounded, responds:*

No you're not! It's an extremely rare disorder!, You can't possibly be obsessive impulsive!

> *Each quickly receives and processes this information and then responds:*

Well—I *am*!

> *Each quickly receives and processes this response and then—incredulous, dumbfounded, and excited—asks:*

You *are*?!

> *Each quickly receives and processes this question and then excitedly answers:*

YES!

> *Each quickly receives and processes this answer and then— incredulous and excited—asks:*

Are you sure?!?

> *Each quickly receives and processes this question and then excitedly answers:*

YES!!

> *Each quickly receives and processes this answer and then, incredulous and skeptical, responds:*

No! No–no–no, you're probably mistaking it with being obsessive compulsive—

> *Each quickly receives and processes what the other has just said and then, puzzled and excited, responds:*

What?—No! I'm *not* [mistaking it with being obsessive compulsive]!,

I'm *not* [mistaking it with being obsessive compulsive]! I'm obsessive *IM*pulsive, I'm obsessive *IM*pulsive!

WOMAN. I've been diagnosed! >

MAN. Me too!

WOMAN. Clinically!

MAN. Me too!

WOMAN. And that's why I just did what I just did to you in the middle of the SuperCen//ter!

MAN. Yeah, and why *I* just did what *I* just did!, I'm obsessive impulsive too!

WOMAN. Have you been diagnosed?!?

MAN. Yes!!

WOMAN. Clinically?!?

MAN. Yes!!!

> *The Man and the Woman kiss—a big, long kiss—at least five seconds.*
>
> *They break away from one another.*

MAN and WOMAN. *(In unison; breathlessly.)* I'm sorry!… It's just that—

> *Quick, earth-shattering discovery.*

—I think I've fallen in love with you at first sight!

> *The Man and the Woman are stunned and overjoyed by this news.*

For real?!? Yeah!! Me too!!

WOMAN. And I keep wanting to kiss you! >

MAN. Me too!

WOMAN. And I'm just acting on that impulse! >

MAN. Yes!

WOMAN. *(Pulling away from the Man.)* And that's something I'm *not* supposed to do. >

MAN. Yeah, I know, I know!

WOMAN. As an obsessive impulsive person, I have to guard *against* that, // acting on *impulse* like that.

MAN. I know, me too, yeah! There's a lot of stuff that, as an obsessive impulsive person, that you've gotta guard against doing—acting on—

MAN and WOMAN. *(In unison.)* —and falling in love—

WOMAN. Yeah!

MAN and WOMAN. *(In unison.)* —especially at first sight—

WOMAN. —yeah!—is one of those things, because of the consequences!, >

MAN. Yeah!

WOMAN. You have to weigh the consequences!, // And—

MAN. Yeah!, And as a clinically diagnosed obsessive impulsive, I'm somehow lacking that capacity to discern consequences.

WOMAN. Exactly!

MAN and WOMAN. *(In unison.)* But: Obsessive Impulsive Disorder *is* treatable

> *[Note: What follows is a rapid recitation of the suggested course of treatment for Obsessive Impulsive Disorder, and its purpose is to explain to the other person that there's hope for improvement. The meaning here is, "I could get better!"]*

through proper diet and exercise, therapy and counseling, medication, and having a loved one watch over you every single moment of the day, >

MAN. *(Indicating where his brother is.)* my brother's over in automotive.	WOMAN. *(Indicating where her sister is.)* my sister's over in home improvement.

MAN and WOMAN. *(In unison; amazed.)* Wow! You really *do* have it, don't you?!?

> *The Man and the Woman kiss again with reckless abandon.*
> *Then:*

WOMAN. *(Breaking away, horrified.)* I'm sorry!

MAN. Yeah, me // too!

WOMAN. That was a lapse, // and >

MAN. Yeah, you don't have to explain!

WOMAN. lapses are gonna happen with me, because my OIR—my Obsessive Impulsive R//atio—

MAN. Obsessive Impulsive Ratio! I know!, You don't have to spell it out for me!, I understand!

WOMAN. Well, my Obsessive Impulsive Ratio is very high, so what keeps happening [all this kissing]—is gonna keep happening, 'cause I've only been in treatment for three years // and—

MAN. Well, that's not a real long time! I've only been in for seven, and my OIR isn't exactly low!

WOMAN. Well, what is it?

MAN. One to thirty-three.*

WOMAN. *(Very impressed.)* Wow! You have an Obsessive Impulsive Ratio of one to *thirty-three*?!?!

MAN. *(A little proud.)* Yeah.

WOMAN. That's *amazing*! >

MAN. Thanks!

WOMAN. Wow!, So for every thirty-three things that you think of to do, that you just…*wanna* do, // you only do—

MAN. Yeah, I only do one now, due largely to the diet and exercise regimen, the therapy and counseling, the medication, and my brother.

WOMAN. Well, that's just great.

MAN. Yeah, but you know, I used to be a one to one!

WOMAN. No!

MAN. Yup!

WOMAN. Me too!

MAN. Really?

WOMAN. Yeah! I did *everything* I thought of to do.

MAN. You'd *think* a thing, you'd *do* it.

WOMAN. Yes!

MAN. Exhausting, isn't it?

WOMAN. You have no idea.

* This is the written-out version of the ratio 1:33.

MAN. I think I do!

WOMAN. Oh! You do!

MAN. Because I understand!!

WOMAN. You understand!!

MAN. I understand!!!

MAN and WOMAN. *(In unison, thrilled to be understood.)* You UNDERSTAND!!! She/he UNDERSTANDS!!!! *(Jumping up and down and joyfully proclaiming to the world:)* SHE/HE UNDER-STANDS ME!!!!!

> *The Man and the Woman are both suddenly mortified, because they realize that they just made quite a scene in the SuperCenter.*

Oh-my-gosh! I'm so sorry about that! I just wanted to jump up and shout to the whole wide world that you understand me because no one ever has before! Who *are* you?!? Where did you *come* from?!? YOU! ARE!! AWESOME!!!

> *And the Man and the Woman have suddenly fallen into a crazy kiss—one that takes them to the floor and all over each other.*
>
> *When they finally stop kissing, they are horrified by their behavior.*

Oh-my-gosh! I'm sorry!

> *The Man and the Woman get up, collect themselves, and apologize to one another profusely—while making sure that no one in the SuperCenter saw what they just did.*

Sorry! >

MAN. Sorry! Sorry...

WOMAN. Sorry about that. *(Relief.)* I don't think anyone saw.

MAN. Yeah, // we're clear!

WOMAN. *(Spotting her sister.)* Oh-my-gosh! >

MAN. What?

WOMAN. I think my sister saw me!—I have to go!

> *The Woman starts to go.*

MAN. No–no–no, // don't go!

WOMAN. No—she only lets me come to the SuperCenter on Friday nights when it seems like I'm getting better, and this is *not* better!, This is [worse!]—

> The Woman realizes that her sister didn't see them kissing.

Wait—!!!

MAN. What?

WOMAN. I don't think she saw!, She's going into *electronics*!!! >

MAN. Oh! [Awesome!]

WOMAN. She didn't *see*!!!

MAN. All right!! So stay!!!

WOMAN. All right!

> The Woman suddenly kisses the Man quickly.

Sorry!

MAN. No! [Don't be!]

> The Man suddenly kisses the Woman—and the kiss almost becomes tender.

> And then the Man suddenly breaks away.

I'm so sorry I keep doing that!

WOMAN. No—it's me! It's me! My OIR is only one to thirteen— you're the one at one to thirty-three! // It's me!

MAN. Hey–hey–hey! Don't compare! You've only been in treatment less than half as long as me—you're doin' great! This is just a rough patch!

WOMAN. I don't know—

MAN. Check this out: There's a guy who's been in treatment for thirteen years—not even twice as long as me—and he has an OIR of one to one billion two hundred and seven million nine hundred and nineteen thousand six hundred and forty-six.

WOMAN. *(In awe.)* Really!

MAN. Yeah.

WOMAN. So he's…normal.

MAN. Yeah. He doesn't do *anything* anymore.

WOMAN. Wow.

MAN. Yeah. So let him inspire you. Stick to the program. It's really good. It's really helped me get my life together.

> *The Man suddenly kisses the Woman—and then breaks away, upset.*

Argh—even though right now it feels like everything's falling apart! >

WOMAN. I know!—

MAN. *(Honest and true.)* Because I really do think I fell in love with you the second I saw you!

WOMAN. Me too!

> *The Woman suddenly kisses the Man quick.*

And, since then, I haven't wanted to do anything except kiss your whole face! That's the only impulse I've had!

MAN. Me too!

> *The Man and Woman kiss each other quick.*

WOMAN. But that's bad.

MAN. Yeah.

> *They kiss each other quick.*

But it doesn't *feel* bad!

WOMAN. No!

> *They kiss each other quick.*

MAN. In fact, it feels *good*!

WOMAN. Yeah!

> *They kiss each other quick.*

Really good!

MAN. Yeah!

> *They kiss each other quick.*

WOMAN. Really–really good!

> *They kiss each other quick.*

MAN. It does, it *does*! (*Suddenly retreating.*) But—wait! I'm not sure it *is* good! Because—remember: Our prescribed plans for wellness don't allow this—for us to fall in love at first sight.

WOMAN. Right, right, // you're right.

MAN. *(Advancing.)* Which is a little confusing to me right now—and really too bad—because I swear: I have fallen in love with you!

WOMAN. Me too, // yeah!

MAN. And not just at first sight—but…for what feels like…could be forever!

WOMAN. *(Advancing.)* Me too, yeah! I mean, *(Advancing.)* I can see myself spending the rest of my life with you!!

MAN. *(Advancing.)* Oh, me too, y//eah!!!

WOMAN. *(Retreating.)* But…that's just not a good idea, >

MAN. *(Retreating.)* You're right.

WOMAN. because we both know—it just won't work, what with the disorder and all.

MAN. I know.

WOMAN. I'll be too much of a burden. >

MAN. Yes [me too]—

WOMAN. A liability even, my sister says.

MAN. Yes, me too, my brother says.

WOMAN. And I don't want to be a burden—or a liability—to anyone other than my sister.

MAN. I understand.

> *Little beat.*

WOMAN. So, I guess I should probably g//o—…

MAN. Yes: Probably the best—the healthiest— >

WOMAN. Yes, yes.

MAN. thing for me to do right now is to just…go.

WOMAN. Yes. Yes. Me, too. Absolutely.

MAN. Yes. So: Very nice to meet you. >

WOMAN. You, too.

MAN. And: Goodbye.

WOMAN. Bye.

> *The Man and the Woman abruptly turn away from each other and start to leave in opposite directions.*

> *Just as abruptly, they stop and turn back to each other, blurting out, in all heartbreaking seriousness.*

MAN and WOMAN. (*In unison.*) I love you!

> *The Man and the Woman are stunned.*

> *And overwhelmed.*

> *That took a lot out of them.*

Oh, no!

WOMAN. I'm sorry!!

MAN. Yeah, // me, too…

WOMAN. I'm sure I didn't mean that!

MAN. Me neither!

WOMAN. Saying something like that can be very misleading!

MAN. Yeah!

WOMAN. One of those lapses!

MAN. Yeah!

> *Little beat.*

> *And then the Man and the Woman suddenly rush to each other to kiss—but the Man stops himself, which stops the Woman.*

> *And the Man decides that a handshake may be more appropriate than a kiss and extends his hand to the Woman.*

> *The Woman looks at the Man's hand…and then takes it… and shakes it.*

Nice to meet you.

WOMAN. You, too.

> *The Man and the Woman start to go.*

> *Lots of sadness.*

MAN and WOMAN. (*Suddenly stopping and turning back to each other; in unison.*) Hey!

*Each eagerly waits to hear what the other has to say before
asking:*

What? [What do you want to say?] Oh [I was just thinking that
maybe we should just make a go of this thing we feel for each other
even though we're not allowed to]—nothin'. Just—...you get better.

Each receives and processes this directive and then responds:

Yeah. You, too.

Little beat.

Bye.*

*The Man and the Woman go their separate ways as the
lights fade.*

Existential space vacuum sound/music/transition.

And we move on to...

---

* Actors and directors: Please see notes on "Obsessive Impulsive" on page 138.

Scene 2: The Singing Telegram

It's 7:30 on the same Friday night in the same alternate suburban reality.

Lights up on the LIVING ROOM of a modest home.

A MAN in full singing telegram regalia arrives.

He knocks on the door.

LOUISE. *(From off.)* Oh, my gosh! Gary?!? You're early!

LOUISE OVERBEE—ebullient, open, passionate, driven, successful, and smart—enters, scrambling to get herself together.

We hear more knocking.

Hold on! It's only 7:30, sweetie! I thought you said be ready at eight?!?

Louise grabs her bag.

We hear more knocking.

I'm comin', I'm comin', cool your jets!

Louise opens the door.

The man dressed in full singing telegram regalia is not who she was expecting to see.

Oh—um… Hello.

SINGING TELEGRAM MAN (STM). *(Cheerily.)* Hello! Singing telegram for Miss Louise Overbee!

LOUISE. Um—I'm sorry—what?

STM. Singing telegram for Miss Louise Overbee!

LOUISE. Wh—? Singing telegram?

STM. Yup. For Miss Louise Overbee, are you Louise Overbee?

LOUISE. Yeah.

STM. Okay, good! Singing telegram for Miss Louise Overbee!

LOUISE. Are you [serious]—? Seriously?

STM. Yeah!

LOUISE. I didn't know they had those anymore, // singing telegrams.

STM. Oh—they do!

LOUISE. Really?!?

STM. Yup.

LOUISE. Okay, um…well, can I see some credentials?

STM. Oh—yeah—sorry—here.

       The Singing Telegram Man presents some sort of identification.

LOUISE. The SuperCenter? >

STM. Yeah—

LOUISE. You work out of the SuperCenter?

STM. Yeah, it's a new service they're providing. They have a kiosk.

LOUISE. Oh. Okay. Well…um… [This is weird.] Who's it from?

STM. Huh?

LOUISE. My singing telegram: Who's it from?

STM. Oh. Um—sorry—this is my first day—um…

       The Singing Telegram Man checks an information card.

…Gary.

LOUISE. *(Super happy and excited.)* GARY?!?!

STM. *(Confused.)* Yeah…

LOUISE. *Really*?!?

STM. Yeah…

LOUISE. Well—… *(Overjoyed.)* What's he—? What is he *doing*?, What is he *up* to?!?

STM. Um, I // don't know.

LOUISE. This is so neato!

STM. Yeah, um, can I ask you somethin' real quick? Who is…Gary?

LOUISE. Oh! He's my guy!

STM. He's [your guy]?!?—

LOUISE. I think we're gonna get married! >

STM. Oh!

LOUISE. And honestly—that's something that I just thought wasn't gonna happen for me, and now— *(JOY!)* —aaaaah!

STM. Well, congratulations!, // Um—

LOUISE. Thanks! I'm lucky. He's pretty great. I mean—get this: Tonight—he's taking me dancing! Isn't that neat?!? For a guy to take a girl dancing on a Friday night, in this day and age?!?

STM. Y//eah!

LOUISE. Yeah! He's always doing stuff like that, always surprising me, and boy, this takes the *cake*!! I mean, a singing *telegram*?!? So *retro*!!!

STM. Yeah!

LOUISE. And so *fun*! So, how do we do this?, I guess just come on in, and…

STM. *(Not wanting to enter Louise's home and sing what he has to sing.)* Oh—u//m—

LOUISE. Where's good?

STM. You know what? I don't want to intrude, so—

LOUISE. You're not intruding!

STM. No, I don't think—

LOUISE. You're not! Now get in here and sing me my singing telegram, Singing Telegram Man!

STM. Well—

LOUISE. *(Insistent.)* Get in here!

STM. O//kay.

> *The Singing Telegram Man reluctantly enters.*

LOUISE. Argh! This is so *FUN*! I mean, what is he *up* to?!?

STM. Um…I'm not sure.

LOUISE. *(Gasping—huge revelation.)* Oh! Oh-my-gosh! Wait! Aaaah! I think I might know what he's up to! Oh-my-[goodness]-aaaaaaaaah! I've been thinking that he might do something like this!, Is he—…Oh, my goodness, I can't breathe—hooooo: Is he *proposing* to me?!? >

STM. Um…

LOUISE. Is that what's happening right now?!?

STM. Well—

LOUISE. Aaaaah! He's proposing, isn't he!! >

STM. Well—

LOUISE.   Aaaaaaah!!!, He's-proposing-he's-proposing-he's-pro-posing-he's PROPOSIIIIIIIIIIIIIIIIING!!!!! AAAAAAAAAH!!!

> *Beat.*

> *Louise is overjoyed and full of anticipation, waiting for the Singing Telegram Man to start singing.*

> *But the Singing Telegram Man is not singing.*

> *He's just standing there, doing nothing.*

Well, don't just stand there! Go ahead! Sing! Sing!! Aaaaaaah! This is so crazy!

STM. Yeah.

> *Beat.*

> *The Singing Telegram Man is frozen.*

LOUISE. What's wrong?

STM. Nothin'.

LOUISE. Are you okay?

STM. Yeah.

LOUISE. Well—then, let's go! Sing!

> *The Singing Telegram Man does nothing.*

Come on! Sing me my singing telegram, Singing Telegram Man!

> *Beat.*

STM. I can't.

LOUISE. What?

STM. I can't do this.

LOUISE. You can't do what?

STM. *(Coming up with an excellent lie to get himself out of the predicament he finds himself in.)* Sing!

LOUISE. What?

STM. I can't sing!

LOUISE. You can't *sing*?!?

STM. Nope!

LOUISE. Of course you can sing, you're a singing telegram man!

STM. No. I can't.

LOUISE. Well—how in the world did you get to be a singing telegram man if you can't sing? >

STM. Um—

LOUISE. How did you get this *job* if you can't sing?!?

STM. Um, well—

LOUISE. I mean, didn't you have to audition?!?

STM. No—

LOUISE. *No?!?*

STM. No, 'cause, see, I guess there's just a real shortage // of us—

LOUISE. There's a *shortage*?!?

STM. Yeah, there's a shortage of singing telegram men right now, // and—

LOUISE. There's a *shortage* of singing telegram men right // now?!?

STM. Yeah, and I guess they just liked me and thought I was pretty charming // and that—

LOUISE. Really.

STM. —yeah—and that I had a lot of charisma, and, so, I think they had the confidence that I could pull it off.

LOUISE. Really.

STM. Yeah, // but—

LOUISE. Well then, pull it off.

STM. Huh?

LOUISE. Pull it off.

STM. But I can't sing.

LOUISE. Tough! It's your *job*, so do your *job*!

STM. But I—

LOUISE. Do your job, Singing Telegram Man!

STM. *(Fear.)* But—

LOUISE. *(Fiercely—and losing it a little.)* Do it!! *I'm excited about this!!! This could be BIG for me!!!!*

STM. *(Finally—and reluctantly—obliging.)* All right, Miss Overbee.

LOUISE. Thank you!

STM. Um…

> *The Singing Telegram Man collects himself…and then continues.*

Okay, um…singing telegram for Miss Louise Overbee from Gary.

LOUISE. *(All starry.)* Aw, Gary. He is somethin' else, isn't he?

STM. Yup. He is.

> *Little beat.*

Well, here goes.

> *The Singing Telegram Man takes out a pitch pipe, finds his note, and sings a song called "No Lie."*

> *"No Lie" is an original song written for this scene. Sheet music is available from Dramatists Play Service.*

> *Here are the lyrics:*

We met and BAM!
You said I was the one.
We have good times.
We have way too much fun.

And now it's time
For me to tell you
Somethin' straight from my heart,
Somethin' that's true.
Now I don't want you to misconstrue,
So listen close cuz this is the truth.

Just like that old song says:
I want you, I need you,
But I ain't ever gonna love you, Louise.
Don't you dare go gettin' down on your knees.
I gotta set myself free.
It's no lie.
I'm sorry if I am makin' you cry.
I never loved you, although I tried.
I gotta be true to me.

I know you thought
You found a love that would last.
I know your heart
Is probably smashed.
But I can't live
This lie anymore.
I need to go my own way.
I'll show myself the door.

Just like that old song says:
I want you, I need you,
but I ain't ever gonna love you, Louise.
Don't you dare go gettin' down on your knees.
I gotta be true to me.
It's no lie.
I'm sorry if I am makin' you cry.
I never loved you, although I tried.
I gotta set us both free.

> *[Note: If you can get the rights, the chorus of "Two Out of Three Ain't Bad" by Meatloaf works really well as the song the Singing Telegram Man sings.]*
>
> *After the Singing Telegram Man sings his song, there is a long, long beat.*
>
> *The awfulness of what just happened washes over Louise.*
>
> *She is devastated.*
>
> *And finally says:*

LOUISE. What the [f*#@ just happened, here]—.

> *A horrible little beat.*

I thought you said you couldn't sing.

STM. Yeah, well—

LOUISE. You sing very well.

STM. Yeah. I can sing fine. I just didn't want to sing *that* to you.

> *Beat.*

LOUISE. Wow. This is—…

The surreal awfulness of what has just happened consumes Louise.

Long beat.

STM. Um…I have another appointment that I have to get to…

The Singing Telegram Man starts to leave.

And then he stops.

Um…

The Singing Telegram Man produces a business card or an information card.

Here's—…um…they ask us to ask you to rate my performance. Here's info on how to do that.

The Singing Telegram Man leaves a business card or an information card somewhere and starts to go.

LOUISE. *(Stopping the Singing Telegram Man.)* What's—?!? Why did he do this?!? Why would anyone do this? What kind of a person… does this—like *this*?

STM. The kind of person I don't think you want to be with.

Little beat.

I'm so sorry.

Little beat.

Goodbye, Miss Overbee.

The Singing Telegram Man starts to go—but stops and turns to Louise…but doesn't say anything…and then leaves.

The lights fade on a sad and perplexed Louise—and on a sad and perplexed Singing Telegram Man, who is just outside her door.

Existential space vacuum sound/music/transition.

And we move on to…

Scene 3: What?!?

It's 7:30 on the same Friday night in the same alternate suburban reality.

Lights up on BEN, standing at the FRONT PORCH or STOOP of a modest home.

He looks great.

He knocks on the door.

He is excited and a little nervous.

Beat.

He knocks again.

Beat.

ANDY answers the door.

BEN. Hey!

ANDY. *(Surprised.)* Hey! Um…what's [up]—? Ooh, nice tie!

BEN. Thanks. // Um—

ANDY. Where'd you get that?

BEN. Online. SuperCenter.

ANDY. Oh. Nice!

BEN. Thanks. Um…

ANDY. I thought [we were on for tomorrow night]—? Isn't it Friday? >

BEN. Yeah—

ANDY. I thought we were on for tomorrow night.

BEN. Yeah, we were, but I couldn't wait. >

ANDY. Oh—

BEN. So I thought I'd surprise ya. >

ANDY. Okay—

BEN. Surprise!

ANDY. Yeah! Um…so…are we doin' something *tonight*, then?

BEN. Yeah. (*Employing some classy innuendo.*) I would like to do some things with you tonight. >

ANDY. Okay.

BEN. (*Employing a little more classy innuendo.*) And tomorrow night, and every night after that. For starters, I wanna come in…

ANDY. U//m—well—

> Andy quickly steps outside, closing the door behind him so that whatever transpires must transpire outside—not inside.

BEN. (*Employing a little more classy innuendo.*) …'cause some of the things I would like to do with you should probably be done… inside.

ANDY. (*Deflecting all the classy innuendo.*) Okay, okay—um, well, Ben: I told you, I can't…do those kinds of things. Yet. I have to take things slow, I // told you—

BEN. I know, and I have totally respected that, but…this is all just *too* slow! It's been over a month now, and I haven't even been inside your place, and you've never been over to mine, and I've never even held your hand, and it's just gettin' a little weird! I mean, are you into this?!?

ANDY. Yeah, // yes!

BEN. Good!, 'Cause I am! *Very*! Into this! And, well…I just think you're great, Andy.

ANDY. I think // you're great, too…

BEN. You're different, and sweet, and not…messed up.

ANDY. Well—

BEN. You're actually decidedly *un*-messed up!

ANDY. Well, I put up a good front.

BEN. But—I feel like…we haven't really moved forward since we met. We're not getting anywhere. And I want to get somewhere! With *you*! Because…

> Ben has something big to say— but can't seem to bring himself to say it.

Argh!—I can't believe—… Argh!—This is crazy!—I never thought I'd be this guy, but—…

Ben struggles to find the words.

ANDY. Are you okay?

BEN.   Yeah— *(Struggling—but still joyful.)* —argh, Andy, listen: Nobody's more surprised by this than I am, but…

> *Ben can't quite say what he says next directly to Andy, so he says it without making eye contact with him.*
>
> *He probably says it to Andy's knees or to the ground—which isn't odd, actually, because the most important things we say are often said without making eye contact.*

I love you.

> *Beat.*
>
> *Andy does not respond to what Ben has just said—because he didn't hear him.*
>
> *He's just looking at Ben, expectantly.*
>
> *Ben reengages with Andy's eyes, hopeful—but wondering why Andy hasn't responded.*

Andy?

ANDY. What?

> *Ben, again, does not make eye contact with Andy and says:*

BEN. I love you, Andy.

> *Andy knows Ben said something—but, again, he didn't hear what he said.*

ANDY. What?

> *Ben reengages with Andy's eyes—and he's probably a little irked.*

BEN. Andy!

ANDY. What? I didn't hear you.

> *Andy really didn't hear Ben.*

BEN. Oh. [Well, that's weird.] Okay. Okay. Well…I mean, again, I know this might be a little soon, but…

> *Ben does not make eye contact with Andy as he says:*

…I think I love you.

> *Andy—again—didn't hear what Ben said.*

ANDY. What?

BEN. *(Irked and hurt.)* Andy! Stop it! Come on, cut it out!

> Little beat; then, simultaneous realizations.

ANDY and BEN. Oh, no! Oh, no!

ANDY. *(To himself.)* Tell me this isn't h//appening!

BEN. You know what? This was a mistake!

ANDY. What was a mistake?

BEN. Forget I said anything.

ANDY. What did you *say*?!?

BEN. Because, obviously, that was way too soon, wasn't it?, // Dammit! >

ANDY. What was too soon?

BEN. *(Starting to leave.)* Stupid! Stupid–stupid–stupid. >

ANDY. *(Not wanting Ben to go.)* Ben—no-no-no!—

BEN. *(Returning.)* But, you know what?, No!! I'm not sorry, and it's not stupid, and I don't care if you're gettin' all *guy* on me here, because I *do*!,

> Ben, again, avoids eye contact—saying what he says next to Andy's knees or to the ground.

I love you, Andy!, // And if—

> Andy does not hear the "I love you" part of what Ben just said.

ANDY. Aaah!, It happened again!, // You *do* what?

BEN. *What* happened again?!?

ANDY. Ben: I didn't hear all of what you just said, so you have to say it // again—

BEN. What?!? Andy, // come on—

ANDY. Ben: Just say what you said again!

BEN. No! And why would I want to?, It hasn't really worked out the way I planned!

ANDY. Because I think I know what you said and I wanna make sure you said it, >

BEN. Andy—

ANDY. and I just need you to say it again!, So just say it again, please!

BEN. Andy—

ANDY. *Please!*

BEN. Andy, no—

ANDY. *Just say it again! PLEASE!*

BEN. All right, relax…

ANDY. And look at me when you do!

BEN. What?

ANDY. *Look at me when you do!!!*

BEN. [This is weird but…] All right, all right…

> *Little beat.*
>
> *Then, Ben makes eye contact with Andy and says:*

I love you.

> *Andy takes in this life-changing information—and is filled with joy.*

ANDY. Oh-my-gosh! Really?

BEN. Yeah. So…you heard me?

ANDY. No—I read your lips.

BEN. What?

> *Andy is overwhelmed—happily so, but also to the point where he may be almost hyperventilating.*

ANDY. Oh-my-gosh!

BEN. What's goin' on? Are you okay?

ANDY. Yeah, yeah—just—… *(Collecting himself.)* Oh, Ben—I'm sorry—I'm so sorry—but—um…

BEN. What?

ANDY. There's this thing about me that might make you think a little differently about the me-not-being-messed-up thing.

BEN. I think I've already started thinking a little differently about the you-not-being-messed-up thing.

ANDY. No—shh! I'm serious. Argh, I should have told you this before: Um, see, I have this thing, um—… Have you ever heard of hysterical blindness?

BEN. No.

ANDY. Well, it's like that.

BEN. I don't know what that's like.

ANDY. Well—they call it conversion disorder now, and…basically what happens is…whenever I undergo emotional stress, that stress manifests itself physically and gets converted into a physical response or symptom, and what you just said there, a second ago—that caused me stress, and so my hearing went.

BEN. That caused *you* stress?!?, >

ANDY. Yeah—

BEN. What I said caused *you* stress?!?

ANDY. Yeah!

BEN. *I'm* the one who said it!!!

ANDY. Yeah, yeah, I know—but…I wasn't *expecting* it! That was just *fast*! And I can't *do* fast! I can only do…slow. Or…incremental.

BEN. Incre//mental?

ANDY. Incremental steps towards joy, yeah, but—

BEN. Incremental steps // towards joy? [What are you talking about??]

ANDY. Towards joy, yeah, but what you did—*said*—there a second ago just…launched me headlong into it, and I am not really capable of handling that.

BEN. Are you serious?

ANDY. Yeah. I can't be dazzled.

BEN. *(Receives and processes.)* What—dazzl//ed?

ANDY. Yeah. My body shuts down when it's dazzled. And, you… dazzle me.

BEN. I [dazzle you]—?

ANDY. Dazzle me, yeah, and it's actually happened before with you: The first time I met you I couldn't actually see you because you're so handsome. Anyway, it's usually minor when it happens, and I've been able to manage it…but what you just said is *major*, and I don't know if I'm gonna be able to manage that, because I know from experience what it'll do to me—

BEN. Wait–wait–whoa—slow down:

> *Little beat.*

Why does this happen?

ANDY. Protection.

BEN. From what?

ANDY. From good stuff, like you.

BEN. What?, What do you need protection from me for? I would never hurt you!

ANDY. Because I *feel* things for you, and—

BEN. That's good!

ANDY. Yeah, but no!, No! It's not! Because—… Because…the first person I ever had feelings for—and who made me feel all the feelings I'm feeling for you right now—well…a lot of people [like my family]…were very disappointed and angry about those feelings— because I was feeling them for a guy. And how disappointed and angry those people [my family] got just…hurt so bad that the next guy I [fell in love with and] felt all these feelings for…well, my body just started shutting stuff down. So I couldn't *have*…those feelings [for guys]—to protect me, they think—I actually collapsed that first time—I had to go to the hospital—and since then…I've just tried not to have those feelings, and I've avoided anything like what we have…and, now, well: Here we are.

BEN. Yeah. Here we are.

ANDY. Yeah. And there's no treatment except to take things as slow as possible—which you have done very well, but—argh—who am I kidding?, *(Getting upset.)* This is gonna be impossible!, You don't need this in your life!, Which is maybe why we should just end this all tonight, right now, >

BEN. What?! No—

ANDY. save us both some trouble, so if you wanna walk away right now, no hard feelings, I get it.

BEN. Whoa–whoa–whoa! I don't wanna walk away.

ANDY. Well, what's—?!? What do you wanna *do*?!?, What do we *do*?!

BEN. We figure this out. 'Cause I love you, Andy, // and—

ANDY. Huh?

> *Ben looks directly at Andy so Andy can read his lips and "hear" him.*

BEN. I love you!

ANDY. Oh, yeah, // right.

BEN. Yeah, and I feel like—what you're saying—is that all the feelings you're feeling…well, I feel like they maybe mean that you feel the same way about me that I feel about you?

ANDY. Oh, I do, Ben!, // I *do*! >

BEN. Well, good!, Then let's [figure this out]—

ANDY. Oh, Ben!, Ah lyuh lyeuoh, too, Ben, but—…

> *[Note: "Ah lyuh lyeuoh" is "I love you," and it should sound like a guttural, animal version of "I love you"—almost like throwing up. It's marred speech—and should sound as if the tongue has gotten paralyzed for a second—and it should be loud, ugly, and unexpected—almost like Andy is possessed. Tip for actor playing Andy: Don't say "Ah lyuh lyeuoh" slowly. Say it at the speed at which you would say, "I love you." Get guttural, ugly, and a little animal. And still make sure that the audience somehow understands that you're saying, "I love you."]*
>
> *Everything stops when Andy says, "Ah lyuh lyeuoh."*
>
> *And then Andy responds to his own strange utterance.*

Oh, no!

> *Andy tries to say "I love you" again, but he can't, because his speech is impaired.*

Ah lyuh lyeuoh, too, Ben, but—…

BEN. Are you // okay?

ANDY. *(Helpless discovery.)* Argh!, My tongue!—My tongue won't let me—argh!—this is what I'm talking about! Ben: Ah lyuh lyeuoh, too, Ben—argh—but, see?!?! >

BEN. *(Understanding what Andy is saying.)* Oh!

ANDY. Ah lyuh lyeuoh, too, Ben! // Ah lyuh lyeuoh, too, Ben!

BEN. Okay, okay! I get it! I get // it!

ANDY. *(Rapid-fire—and loud, ugly, guttural, and desperate to be heard and understood.)* AH-LYUH-LYEUOH-TOO, AH-LYUH-LYEUOH-TOO, AH-LYUH-LYEUOH-TOO, // AH-LYUH-LYEUOH-TOO, BEN!

BEN. Okay, okay! I get it! Stop talking!, Stop talking!

> *Everything is quiet for a moment as Ben understands— happily!—what's happening.*

All right. This is good! A little not-quite-what-I-planned…but this is good!

ANDY. No!, It's not!

BEN. Yes, it is! This was…a big step we just took!

ANDY. Yeah, and that's—I can't do that! I can't take big steps!

BEN. All right. Then…we'll take small ones.

> *Ben holds out his hand, offering it for Andy to hold—like you would if you were about to go on a walk with someone you love.*

Here.

ANDY. What are you doing?

BEN. Taking small steps. Take my hand.

ANDY. I can't—

BEN. Take it.

ANDY. But I don't know what'll happen to me if I do that. My nervous system might [shut down]—

BEN. I don't know what'll happen to me. So just take it. And let's go for a walk.

> *Ben offers Andy his hand again.*
>
> *Andy looks at Ben's hand.*
>
> *And the lights fade.*
>
> *Existential space vacuum sound/music/transition.*
>
> *And we move on to…*

Scene 4: The Answer

It's 7:30 on the same Friday night in the same alternate suburban reality.

Lights up on tuxedo-clad KEITH, sitting on the toilet—lid down!—in the BATHROOM.

CELIA appears outside the bathroom in a wedding dress.

She goes to the door and knocks, but doesn't try to open it yet.

CELIA. Babe?

KEITH. *(Relieved; going to the door, but not opening it yet.)* Oh, thank God! Celia! Hey!—

CELIA. Hey! The guys said you wanted to…talk to me?

KEITH. Yeah—I'm sorry, I'm so sorry.

CELIA. It's okay., It's okay. People are just…you know…wondering if they should stay or go.

KEITH. What—no—!

CELIA. Should they stay?

KEITH. Yes, they should stay! Of course they should stay!

CELIA. Okay, good!

> *Little beat.*

So…what's goin' on?, You okay?

KEITH. Yeah, yeah. It's just—I was just standing up there in front of all those people—you were just about to walk down the aisle and all—and…

CELIA. What?

KEITH. I don't know—I just thought I was gonna be sick, you know?—My stomach.—So I came up here.

CELIA. Okay.

KEITH. 'Cause I guess it just hit me how *big* this is!

CELIA. Well, it *is* big.

KEITH. Yeah!

Little beat.

CELIA. Um…can I come in so we can talk about this?

Celia starts to open the door, which Keith quickly slams shut—and locks.

KEITH. No! You can't come in here! I can't see the bride on the wedding day till the wedding part, you know that! >

CELIA. Keith—

KEITH. And you can't see the groom! It's bad luck!

CELIA. Well, yeah, if you believe in that sort of thing!

KEITH. Well, I'm not taking any chances!

CELIA. Keith—

KEITH. Wait–wait–wait: You know what?! Make a blindfold!

CELIA. *(Receives and processes.)* What?

KEITH. Make a blindfold! I'm gonna make one, too! >

CELIA. Keith—

KEITH. Hold on!

Keith grabs a roll of toilet paper for Celia to make a blindfold out of.

Okay: I'm gonna open the door—but don't look at me—and I'm gonna hand you some toilet paper.

CELIA. What?

Keith opens the door just enough so he can hand Celia the toilet paper so she can make herself a blindfold—but not enough that they can see each other.

KEITH. Just take this [the toilet paper roll]! And wrap it around your head like a blindfold so you can't see me. I'm gonna make one, too, so I can't see you!

CELIA. Babe!—

KEITH. Do it! 'Cause we can't see each other on the wedding day till the wedding part, and I really need to talk to you!

CELIA. *(Amused and a little irked.)* Okay.

Celia takes the toilet paper roll, and Keith closes the bathroom door as soon as she does.

And then Celia uses the toilet paper to make herself a blind-
fold while Keith makes himself a blindfold with his tie.

KEITH. Tell me when you're done. Are you done?

CELIA. No—hold on—give me a sec!

Keith finishes making his blindfold.

KEITH. Well, tell me when you're done! I'm done!, Are you done?

CELIA. Hold on…

KEITH. Are you done now?

CELIA. Keith! Almost—

Celia finishes making her blindfold.

Yeah—yes—I'm done.

KEITH. All right.

Keith goes to the door.

Are you sure?!

CELIA. Yes!

KEITH. Okay!

Keith opens the door, gropes for Celia, finds her, pulls her into
the bathroom, slams the door shut, and hugs her desperately.

Oh, I'm sorry, // I'm so sorry!

CELIA. Hey-hey-hey! It's okay! It's okay!

KEITH. Oh, it's so, so good to see you!

CELIA. Well, it's so, so good to…"see"…you, too.

KEITH. Oh, I love you so much!

CELIA. I love you, too!

KEITH. Oh, I'm *so* sorry…it's just…this is a lot of *pressure*, you
know? >

CELIA. Yeah, // but—

KEITH. I mean, the *expectations*! That we're just gonna live happily
ever after?!? When everybody knows that this is a *risk* we're taking!
I mean, we're setting ourselves up for *failure*!, >

CELIA. What?

KEITH. 'Cause chances are we're not gonna make it, you know!

CELIA. What? // Why do you [say that]—?

KEITH. 'Cause over fifty percent of all marriages end in divorce, right? Isn't that the statistic?

CELIA. Keith! What—?!?

KEITH. And what if you end up hating me?!?

CELIA. Keith! I'm // never gonna *hate* you!

KEITH. I mean, you've *seen* it: Married people who *hate* each other?, We've all seen that! >

CELIA. Keith—

KEITH. It's so *latent*! And *awful*! But I get it. Especially in women, because women give up more when they get married. To men, I mean., I mean—your *names*!!, You give up your *names* right out of the gate!

CELIA. But…I'm not doing that! I'm keeping my name!

KEITH. Well, yeah, but you're gonna be doing more housework than you've ever done before, // because >

CELIA. Wha—?!?

KEITH. that's what happens! Husbands create seven extra hours of housework a week for their wives: That's a fact!, I read that!, And I don't want to be that guy!

CELIA. Keith! You're not gonna be that guy, because I'm not gonna let you be that guy! And anyway, I'm the messy one! We've lived together for three years, and I'm the one who makes more housework for you!

KEITH. Celia: You're not listening to me. I asked you a question, and you didn't answer it. What if *this* [us, married]…doesn't work?

CELIA. What if what doesn't work?

KEITH. Us. You and me. Married.

CELIA. When did you ask me that?

KEITH. When you came in here.

CELIA. No, you didn't. >

KEITH. Yes, I did.

CELIA. You never asked me that.

KEITH. Well, I'm asking you now!: What if we get married…and we can't make it work? What'll we do?

CELIA. Keith—I don't know—…

> *Celia struggles to answer such an ill-timed question.*

I really don't want to think about this // right now!

KEITH. Split up?

CELIA. I don't know…

KEITH. Get a divorce?

CELIA. I—…I guess.

KEITH. Just like that?!?

CELIA. *(Struggling to make sense of what Keith is saying.)* Yeah, if that's what we want, yeah, // but I—

KEITH. Well, that's not something I'm ever gonna *want*!!!

CELIA. Well, me // neither!!

KEITH. I don't want to get *divorced*!!

CELIA. Well, let's *not*, // then!

KEITH. We have to promise each other right now that when we get married we will *never* get divorced!!

CELIA. All right!, I promise! That's kinda what today // is all about!

KEITH. No—but wait: If we do that…then we'd be stuck with each other!

CELIA. *Keith*!?! What're you [talking about]—? Babe: I *want* to be stuck with you.

> *Beat.*
>
> *Realization.*

The question right now seems to be…do *you*…want to be stuck… with *me*?

> *Keith thinks.*
>
> *And then gasps.*
>
> *And then has a joyful revelation.*

KEITH. Oh-my-gosh!

CELIA. What?

KEITH. Oh-my-gosh!!

CELIA. *What*?

KEITH. That's what this is! That's what this is all about!!

CELIA. What?, What what's all about?

KEITH. I never...*answered*...that question!

CELIA. Huh?

KEITH. I never answered you, when you asked me to marry you!

CELIA. Yes, you did!

KEITH. No, I didn't! I just...stood there all stupid, 'cause you //
surprised the heck out of me!

CELIA. Yeah, but then you giggled and picked me up and hugged
me and spun me around!

KEITH. Yeah, and the next thing I know, we're just doing all the
things people do when they decide to get married—the invitations,
you're trying on dresses, checking out bands and venues—which
we didn't like any of, so we decided to do it here, in the house we
bought together.

CELIA. Yeah! And all that wasn't...YES?

KEITH. No, 'cause I didn't *say* it!

CELIA. Yes, you did!

KEITH. When?

CELIA. *(Pondering.)* Well—

KEITH. Do you remember hearing me say YES?

CELIA. Well, I don't know... No, I guess // not, but—

KEITH. No, you don't, because I didn't say it! And I want to! I
wanna say YES!

CELIA. Well then say YES, and let's go do this!

KEITH. All right, well, then ask me again!!

CELIA. What?—

KEITH. Ask me again right now! If I'll marry you! Like you did
that night—that beautiful late September Friday night just like this
one, so I can say YES!

CELIA. Sweetie—

KEITH. I wanna say YES, Celia! I need to say YES! So ask me again!, Please!, Now!

CELIA. Okay, okay.

KEITH. Thank you.

CELIA. Just—here—

Celia goes to take Keith's makeshift blindfold off.

KEITH. *(Feeling Celia groping for his blindfold.)* What are you doing?!?

CELIA. Taking our blindfolds off—

KEITH. *(Stopping Celia.)* No! // Stop! No!

Celia tries to take Keith's blindfold off repeatedly throughout what follows.

Keith thwarts Celia's every attempt.

CELIA. Yes, so I can look in your eyes and >

KEITH. No–no!

CELIA. ask you if you'll marry me >

KEITH. No–no!

CELIA. like I did that night!

KEITH. No! No! Don't! 'Cause when I say YES, then we will have seen each other on our wedding day before the wedding part, and that's bad luck!

Little beat.

Celia is amused and exasperated by Keith's behavior.

CELIA. All right…

Little beat.

Celia gets down on bended knee and takes Keith's hands in hers.

Keith Goodwin: I know this isn't the way this is typically done… but nothing about us is very typical…and so: I love you…and…

Celia says nothing else—because she can't seem to.

She seems confused.

Beat.

Keith is confused by—but not yet concerned about—the silence.

KEITH. Babe?

CELIA. Sorry! Um—…

Celia collects herself.

Keith is joyful, anticipating the happily-ever-after that's about to ensue.

I love you…and…

Celia says nothing else.

And thinks.

And, after a beat, she pulls away from Keith, rips off her blindfold, and stares at her groom.

KEITH. Celia?

Keith senses that something's wrong and rips his blindfold off.

And their eyes meet for the first time today.

And maybe for the first time in a long time.

What's wrong?

Little beat.

Celia?

Beat.

CELIA. I—…

A realization.

Then, stone cold dead serious.

I can't do this.

KEITH. What?

CELIA. I can't ask you [to marry me]…again…because—… Oh, Keith:

A more painful realization.

I don't want you to say YES.

KEITH. What?

CELIA. I don't want this.

Long, long beat.

I'm sorry, I'm so sorry—

KEITH. No. It's okay. 'Cause…

Keith has his own painful realization.

…I don't either.

CELIA. What?

Long, long, long beat—of disbelief.
This is completely uncharted territory.
Then, suddenly:

But—wait: I love you!

KEITH. Me, too!

CELIA. I really // do!

KEITH. I love you, too!

Long, long, long, painful beat of confusion.

CELIA. What do we do?!?

KEITH. I don't know.

Long, long, long unbearable beat as Keith searches for an
answer to Celia's question—and finally comes up with one.

I guess…we should go tell everybody.

CELIA. What? What do we tell them?

KEITH. I don't know.

Keith searches for an answer to Celia's question—and finally
comes up with a lame one.

Somethin'.

Beat.

Lights fade as Celia and Keith take each other by the hand
and figure out how to go and tell everybody their news.

Existential space vacuum sound/music/transition.

And we move on to…

Scene 5: Uh-Oh

It's 7:30 on the same Friday night in the same alternate suburban reality.

Lights up on BILL and SARAH in the STUDY.

Bill is wearing earbuds—watching episode three of season four of a very funny comedy on his iPad.

Sarah reads from her iPad.

Bill enjoys what he's watching—loudly.

Sarah is irked by this.

She looks at Bill disdainfully.

Then she looks away.

Then she thinks.

Then she looks at her husband again.

And then gets his attention—maybe by giving him a little kick or a tap.

SARAH. Hey! Bill!

BILL. *(De-earbudding.)* Yeah?

> *Sarah is full of something to say…but decides not to say it and instead says, laughing:*

SARAH. Nothin'.

> *Sarah goes back to her iPad, smiling to herself, and Bill re-earbuds—and enjoys what he is watching—even more.*
>
> *Sarah is irked by her husband's enjoyment.*
>
> *And she looks at him disdainfully.*
>
> *And then she looks away from him and thinks.*
>
> *And then she looks at him again and taps him again.*

Bill?

BILL. *(De-earbudding.)* Yeah?

> *Sarah is full of something to say again…but again decides not to say it and instead smiles and says:*

SARAH. Nothin'.

BILL. You sure?

SARAH. *(Totally convincing.)* Yeah! Yeah–yeah–yeah!

> *Sarah goes back to her iPad and Bill re-earbuds—and enjoys what he's watching—even more.*
>
> *Sarah is irked by her husband's enjoyment—again.*
>
> *And she looks at him disdainfully.*
>
> *And then she looks away from him and thinks.*
>
> *And then she looks at him again and taps him again.*

Bill?

BILL. *(De-earbudding—and getting irritated by Sarah's interruptions.)* Honey, what?!?

> *Sarah is full of something to say again…but again decides not to say it and instead smiles and says:*

SARAH. Nothing.

BILL. Well, I'm watching something, here!, Let me watch!, Shh!

> *Sarah does not appreciate having just been shushed by her husband.*
>
> *And is a little taken aback.*
>
> *And a little furious.*
>
> *She stares at Bill while he re-earbuds and resumes watching whatever he's watching.*
>
> *Bill continues to laugh at and love what he's watching.*
>
> *And, finally, Sarah has had it and decides to say what's really on her mind.*
>
> *And she gives Bill a little kick or smack to get his attention and says:*

SARAH. Hey! Bill!

BILL. *(Exasperated, de-earbudding.)* Honey, what?!?

> *Little beat.*

SARAH. Just…

> *Sarah doesn't say what's on her mind and instead smiles and says:*

I love you!

BILL. Well, I love you, too!, What's goin' on? >

SARAH. Nothing!

BILL. Are you okay?

SARAH. Yeah!, Yeah! I just…

BILL. What?

SARAH. Well…just—… Can I ask you something?

BILL. Yeah.

SARAH. *(Really asking the question.)* How long does it feel like we've been married?

BILL. *(Receives and processes.)* What? How long does it fe//el like we've been married?

SARAH. …feel like we've been married—yeah—to you, yeah.

BILL. Um…well, about a year and a half, because // that's how—

SARAH. That's how long it feels like we've been married, to you, about a year and a half?

BILL. Um…yeah, because that's how long we've been married. Best year and a half of my life!

SARAH. Aw! [That's sweet.]

BILL. Why do // you ask?

SARAH. *(Little explosion.)* Wow! Only *one* little year. And a *half* of another one, huh?!?

BILL. Yeah.

> *Little beat.*

Does it feel…longer to you or something?

SARAH. What?!? No!—Wait: UH-OH: Yeah—it does—maybe. A little.

BILL. What do you mean?

SARAH. Well, Bill:

> *Beat.*

> *Sarah tries to figure out how to put what she is about to say delicately.*

I'm…*bored.*

BILL. Oh.

SARAH. Yeah. I mean—it's a Friday night, and look at us. We're just sitting here. You're watching something, I'm reading something.

BILL. I thought we liked reading. And watching stuff.

SARAH. Well—we do, but I'm bored, and being bored at this stage of the game—I mean, a year and a half *in*—is not what I hoped and dreamed, honestly.

BILL. Okay.

SARAH. Yeah, I feel like I'm *languishing.*

BILL. *(Receives and processes.)* Languishing?

SARAH. Yeah, and I don't wanna languish. I wanna have *fun* and do exciting *things*!

BILL. Okay. Okay, okay. Honey: I think I might know what this is. You're just—I think—… You know what? This is just what happens.

SARAH. Huh?

BILL. Yeah—I was just reading about this somewhere…

> *Bill does a quick search on his iPad.*

Argh, I can't remember where—I'll send you the link—but…there was a big study done recently about how after the first year/year and a half of marriage—the "honeymoon period" they call it—romance and passion can fade a little, and—when that happens—couples just have to work a little harder to figure out how to rekindle whatever it is they've lost, and the best way to do that—the study said—is for them to try to find the "fun" again. And maybe we just need to… find the fun again.

SARAH. Oh! Yeah! Maybe we do!

> *Little beat.*

So let's find it!

BILL. Huh?

SARAH. Let's find the fun again! Right now! You first!, Find the fun!, Go!

BILL. Well, honey, you know what? I don't really feel like we've *lost* the fun, actually—

SARAH. Well, *I* do.

BILL. Well…can we find it tomorrow? I've had a long week, and I just wanna // watch my show—

SARAH. I don't think I can wait that long.

BILL. Oka//y—

SARAH. Yeah, I need to find the fun *now*.

BILL. Oka//y.

SARAH. Because I don't wanna be *bored*, because being *bored*…well, it's just not good for people., Do you think it's good for people? >

BILL. No—

SARAH. 'Cause I don't think it is., 'Cause, see, I was just reading something, too, here, actually…

Sarah does a quick search on her iPad.

Argh, I can't find it, but it was in an article—in a journal somewhere—that was written about a study that was done by *experts* on people who just can't. Be. Bored.

BILL. Oh?

SARAH. Yeah, it's about how there are people in this world who just can't *help* themselves but take extreme *action* when // they get bored, and—

BILL. Wait, "extreme action"?

SARAH. Yeah.

BILL. Like what? Like skydive, bungee jump, bullfight—?

SARAH. No, like kill.

BILL. What?!?

SARAH. Kill. The theory is that that's what they'll do when they're bored: Kill.

BILL. *What*?!?

SARAH. Kill. In the cases cited in the article, kill the people they love most.

BILL. Wha—*No*!!

SARAH. Yeah. Because their hopes and dreams haven't been fulfilled. It's a [psychological] *(Pointing to her head.)* thing. >

BILL. Really?

SARAH. They call it—argh!—I can't remember what it's called, but there are people who have this [psychological] *thing,* // and—

BILL. Well, like people like who?

SARAH. Well, like people in prison.

BILL. Really?

SARAH. Yeah!

BILL. I had no idea.

SARAH. Yeah, it's a [psychological] *thing,* and, well—I was just thinking:

> *Little beat.*

> *And then Sarah really, truly asks:*

What if *I* was one of those people? What if when I got bored, I *killed*? I killed *you.*

> *Little beat.*

> *And then Sarah really, truly asks:*

What would you do?

BILL. Um—…

SARAH. *(Really, truly asking.)* Would you stay with me?

BILL. *(Considering.)* I—. I—…

SARAH. *(Matter-of-factly.)* Yeah, it's a tough one. 'Cause if you *stayed,* I'd probably kill you, 'cause I'm bored. But if you *left,* you'd be a promise-breaker, because we *are* married, and you *did* promise to stay with me in good times and in *bad,* for better or for *worse,* in sickness and in health, and—if you *left* me, you'd be breaking a vow.

> *Little beat.*

That's a tough one. You'd kinda end up losing either way.

> *Little beat.*

What would you do?

BILL. *(Receives and processes.)* Um…well…I'd like to think that—A) that something like this would never happen, and B)…that…I'd stay. Because I love you. And because we'd be dealing with mental illness. And you'd need my help in dealing with that, so, yeah: I'd stay. And help you get better. Help you…not be bored.

SARAH. If you *knew* I was gonna kill you, you'd stay?

BILL. I think I would.

SARAH. Really?

BILL. Yeah.

SARAH. Really?

BILL. Yeah. I can't imagine my life without you, s//o…

SARAH. Aw, that's really sweet of you, Bill.

> *Sarah gives Bill a quick kiss.*
>
> *All is well!*
>
> *And Bill resumes watching his show.*
>
> *And then…Sarah gets her bag or reaches into a drawer and produces…a gun—which she points at Bill with conviction and authority and know-how.*
>
> *Eventually, Bill notices that his wife is pointing a gun at him.*

BILL. What the—…? Honey…

> *Bill kind of puts his hands up because…what else do you do?*

What are you doing?

SARAH. *(Totally earnest and reasonable discovery.)* Bill: I think I'm one of those people who kills the people they love most when they're bored, and I never-ever-ever-ever-ever thought I'd get bored with you, with us, with things, but I did: UH-OH.

BILL. *(Receives and processes.)* What?!? You're—one of those people?

SARAH. Yeah.

BILL. Well, how do you know?

SARAH. I took a test. They had one of those tests, "Could You Kill?: A Personality Test," at the end of the article. And I did really well on it.

Or—poorly. Anyway, I answered all the questions "right." I have all
the symptoms. And it said that I. Could. Kill. [Amazing, right?]

BILL. Oh.

SARAH. Yeah.

> *Little beat.*

How 'bout that, huh?

BILL. How 'bout that.

> *Beat.*
>
> *Bill pleads.*

Sarah…

> *Bill tries to leave.*

SARAH. *(Reasonably and matter-of-factly.)* Oh, n-n-no! Don't you
go, Bill! You're not *going*, are you? You said you wouldn't! You just
said you'd *stay* with me! And help me get better!

BILL. Yeah, when this was all hypothetical!, Where did you get
a gun?!?

SARAH. At the SuperCenter.

BILL. Oh.

SARAH. To keep us safe. From the outside.

BILL. Oh.

SARAH. It's dangerous out there.

BILL. Yeah…

> *Beat.*
>
> *A standoff.*
>
> *Then, another plea.*

Sarah: I love you, Sarah! Sarah, please…

> *Sarah shoots Bill.*

SARAH. BAM!

> *Bill screams as Sarah shoots Bill several more times—fast.*
>
> *Bam-bam-bam-bam-bam-bam-bam-bam-bam!*
>
> *Eventually, Bill learns that Sarah is shooting him with a
> WATER GUN!*

And this should be a total surprise—to Bill and to the audience!

Bill is soaked.

[Note: Make sure the actor playing Bill is wearing a shirt that shows the water stain well. A medium light blue shade seems to work well.]

Sarah explodes with laughter.

She has pulled off the best practical joke ever!

And she is THRILLED!

HAHAHAHAHAHAHAHA!! I got you so bad! HAHAHAHA!!! It's not *real*! It's a squirt gun! It's not *real*! I got you so *bad*!!! Oh, my goodness!, Your *face*! *Hilarious*! You thought I was gonna *kill* you?!?! I'm not gonna *kill* you! I'm your *WIFE*! I *LOVE* you! I'm not gonna *kill* you!

BILL. *(Distraught.)* Sarah!!!

SARAH. Oh, Bill! Baby, I was just *playin'*! I made the whole thing *up*! There's no such *study*! No…*test*! People who kill the people they love most when they're *bored*?!? People don't do things like that! And if they do—well, they're *crazy*! And I'm not *crazy*! I would never do something like that! I'm sorry! Come here!

    Sarah goes to comfort Bill, but Bill recoils and cowers.

Oh, baby, come on! I'm sorry! I'm so sorry! I was just trying to wake us up, shake things up, to help us find the fun again! You gotta find the fun in a marriage or it'll fizzle!

BILL. Yeah, well, that wasn't really very fun for me.

SARAH. Oh, baby, come on! I was just playin', silly goose!

    Sarah squirts Bill again, playfully.

BILL. *(Distraught.)* Sarah!:

    Bill takes a beat to sort through what has just happened.

    And then asks the hard question:

Do I…bore you? >

SARAH. No!

BILL. So much that you wanna kill me?

SARAH. No! Bill! Don't // be silly!

BILL. And is our life…not what you hoped and dreamed?!?

SARAH. Well, not exactly—but it's okay: >

BILL. Whoa—

SARAH. I've learned to adjust my expectations. [Whoops.] >

BILL. *What*?!? >

SARAH. I mean—

BILL. You shouldn't have to do that! *I* haven't had to do that! You've fulfilled *my* expectations! *Exceeded* them, even, and I want to fulfill yours! *Exceed* them, even!

SARAH. *(Stone cold dead serious.)* All right. Then do it. Fulfill, exceed, right now, go.

BILL. Well, I don't…feel like I know how to do that right now.

SARAH. Bill: How 'bout just…*try*.

BILL. Okay.

SARAH. And keep trying.

BILL. Oka//y.

SARAH. Every day.

BILL. Oka//y.

SARAH. And never stop.

BILL. Oka//y.

SARAH. Ever.

BILL. Okay.

SARAH. *(Pointing the squirt gun at him.)* Till the day you die.*

> *Lights fade—or maybe this is a blackout.*
> *Existential space vacuum sound/music/transition.*
> *And we move on to…*

---

* See notes on "Uh-Oh" on page 139..

Scene 6: Lunch and Dinner

It's 7:30 on the same Friday night in the same alternate suburban reality.

Lights up on KELLY in the BEDROOM.

She is just home from work and has probably just changed her clothes and might be putting her work clothes away.

She is doing very important things on her phone.

We hear MARK, Kelly's husband, enter the house.

MARK. *(Calling to his wife, from off.)* Honey! I'm home!!

KELLY. *(Calling to her husband.)* Hey! I'm in here!

Beat.

Mark enters the bedroom, doing very important things on his phone.

MARK. Hey.

KELLY. Hey.

Mark gives Kelly a routine coming-home-from-work kiss.

They barely look at each other as they kiss, because they're both buried in their phones and lost in their respective coming-home-from-work routines.

In what follows, Mark takes off his shoes, loosens his tie, unbuttons his shirt—all the while checking his phone.

While neither Kelly nor Mark pays much attention to the other, absolutely nothing is wrong.

This is a settled, content couple.

All is well.

Until it isn't.

MARK. How was your day?

KELLY. Great! Crazy, but it's Friday!

MARK. Yay, Friday!

KELLY. How was yours?

MARK. Great! Crazy—but it's Friday!

KELLY. Yay, Friday!

Beat.

Kelly is buried in her phone.

Mark is buried in his.

MARK. Hey, how was your deposition?

KELLY. Oh, super!

MARK. Glad to hear it.

Beat.

Mark is buried in his phone.

Kelly is buried in hers.

KELLY. Oh, how was your presentation?

MARK. Went excellent.

KELLY. Awesome.

Beat.

Mark is buried in his phone.

Kelly is buried in hers.

MARK. Oh, how was your luncheon?

KELLY. Huh?

MARK. You had a luncheon today, // didn't you?

KELLY. Oh, yeah, // yeah.

MARK. How was it?

KELLY. Really good!

MARK. Good, what'd you have?

KELLY. Hm?

MARK. For lunch, at the luncheon?

KELLY. Oh, sex.

Kelly says this nonchalantly, still buried in her phone.

And she says it as if she were saying she had a BLT.

Mark finally really looks at Kelly and takes in what she just said.

MARK. What?

KELLY. *(Still buried in her phone.)* Sex.

> *Kelly thinks she's telling Mark what she actually had for lunch.*

MARK. What?!?

KELLY. Sex, had sex for lunch, it was really good.

> *Again, Kelly thinks she's simply telling Mark what she actually had for lunch—and that it was really good.*
>
> *After a beat, Kelly slowly comes to realize what she has just said—but she is not about to admit that she said what she just said, and she covers extremely well and smiles and says:*

I mean…*salmon*! I had *salmon*! They had chicken, beef, salmon, and a vegetarian option, and I had the salmon!, It was really terrific salmon—had a nice little mango sauce!

> *Mark takes in this information, trying to figure out what is happening.*

MARK. Hone//y—

KELLY. *(Moving on, grabbing her work clothes, putting them on a hanger, and exiting to hang them up in the closet.)* What'd *you* have? You didn't have a luncheon, did you?

MARK. No—

KELLY. *(From off.)* No, I didn't think so, so what'd you have?, // For lunch?

MARK. *(More to himself than to her.)* A meatball sub.

KELLY. Huh?

MARK. I had a meatball sub.

KELLY. *(Returning.)* Was it good?

MARK. It was oka//y…

KELLY. Great!

> *Kelly aggressively occupies herself with some sort of activity to deflect—like lotioning. (Lotioning aggressively is very funny.)*
>
> *Little beat.*

MARK. Honey, can we just go back for a second? Did you just say that you had *sex* for lunch? Is that what you just said?

KELLY. No! [Are you crazy?!?]

MARK. Um…I think you did.

KELLY. No, // I said—

MARK. No, I think you did.

KELLY. No, // I said—

MARK. No—you did!

KELLY. No! // I said I had salmon!

MARK. No, you did—twice—three times—no *four*! Four times!! After I asked you how your day was and how your deposition was, I asked you what you had for lunch at your luncheon, and you said, "Sex," and I said, "What?," and you said, "Sex," and I said, "What?," and you said, "Sex, had sex for lunch, it was really good."

> *Little beat.*

Why did you say that?!?

KELLY. *(Laughing off her slipup.)* Well, honey, I don't know—I mean, I had *salmon*! I didn't have sex for lunch at the luncheon!, I mean, who has that for lunch at a luncheon?! >

MARK. I don't know, Kelly—

KELLY. What kind of a thing is that for a person to have for lunch at a luncheon?!

MARK. *(Starting to lose it.)* I don't know, Kelly, what kind of a thing *is* that for a person to have for lunch at a luncheon, huh?!?

> *Beat.*
>
> *Kelly busies herself with her phone or with some tidying up. (Or maybe she starts to go, and Mark stops her with:)*

Kelly!!: Why did you say that?!?

KELLY. Well—honey—I don't know.

MARK. You don't *know*? What do you mean you don't know?

KELLY. It just…it slipped, I guess.

MARK. It slipped?

KELLY. Yeah—

MARK. *(Getting worked up.)* It *slipped*, you guess?!?

KELLY. Yeah, and don't get all worked up, 'cause it was nothing, //
I promise. >

MARK. What was nothing?!?

KELLY. It was just what they had!

MARK. Just what they *had*?!?

KELLY. Yeah, for lunch at the luncheon!

MARK. Just what *w//ho* had?

KELLY. *(A discovery that will eventually lead to the truth.)* And it
was really good!

MARK. What do you mean it was really good?!?

KELLY. *(Another discovery that will eventually lead to the truth.)* It
was different than the way you make it!

MARK. Make what?

KELLY. Love!— >

MARK. Kelly!!

KELLY. *(Retreating back into denial of the truth.)* Argh! *Lunch!,
Lunch!*, I mean *lunch*!

MARK. I don't think you *do* [mean lunch]!!!

KELLY. And besides, like I said, it was nothing!

MARK. What // was nothing?!?

KELLY. It was nothing!, It was nothing!, It was nothing! It was
just—…

    Kelly searches for a way to defend herself.

MARK. *WHAT*?!?

KELLY. I was just—…I was *HUNGRY*!!!

MARK. *(Receives and processes.)* You were *hungry*?!?

KELLY. Ye//ah!

MARK. You were *hungry*?!?

KELLY. Yeah!

MARK. *(Exploding.)* Well, then…*have a SANDWICH*!!!

    Beat.

    Everything settles.

Kelly, *WHO*?!? Who did you have sex for lunch with?!?

KELLY. Oh, honey, I don't even know…

MARK. You don't even *know*?!?, >

KELLY. No—

MARK. You don't *know*?!?

KELLY. No—

MARK. What do you mean you don't *know*?!?

KELLY. Just that! And besides, it doesn't matter.

MARK. It doesn't *matter*?!?

KELLY. Yeah, 'cause it was just what they *had*, >

MARK. Why do you keep saying that?!?

KELLY. *(An explosive blurt.)* and it looked really good and I hadn't had any for a long time, and *SO I HAD SOME*!!!

> *Beat.*
>
> *Everything settles.*
>
> *The truth is out.*

MARK. Kelly, you haven't had any for a long time because you don't let me near you anymore.

KELLY. What?!? That's not right!

MARK. I know!

KELLY. No! I mean you've got it wrong!

MARK. What?

KELLY. You don't let *me* near *you*!

MARK. No!

KELLY. Yes! Every time I try to get near you, you shrink!

MARK. What?!?

KELLY. You shrink!

MARK. I *shrink*?!?

KELLY. Yeah—[you shrink] away from me! And you make a face!

MARK. I do not!

KELLY. You *do*!

MARK. No, *you* shrink and *you* make a face when I try to get near *you*!

KELLY. No, *you* do that!, *You* do that!, Every time I try to seduce you!

MARK. Every time you try to *seduce* me?!?

KELLY. Yes!

MARK. Kelly: Honey: I can't remember the last time you tried to seduce me!

> *Beat.*
>
> *A standoff.*
>
> *Then, a huge realization.*

Are you [having an affair]—…?!? Kelly, are you having an affair?!? >

KELLY. No!

MARK. You're having an affair, aren't you?!? >

KELLY. I'm not!!

MARK. Are you having an affair?!?

KELLY. No!! >

MARK. Answer me!!!

KELLY. I'm not having an *affair*!!!

> *Beat.*
>
> *A standoff.*
>
> *Mark puts his shoes back on and starts to go.*

What are you doing?

MARK. I'm—…

> *Mark stops, turns to his wife, and what he says next is loaded.*
>
> *He's playing what he thinks is her game now.*

I'm…*hungry*. I want something for *dinner*. And I'm thinking of going out for it. For my *dinner*.

> *Mark starts to go.*
>
> *Kelly realizes what Mark means and stops him with:*

KELLY. No! Mark! Wait—please don't do that! Please don't go! Please!

MARK. Well, it's dinnertime, and I gotta eat, 'cause let me tell ya: I'm *very hungry*.

KELLY. Okay: I understand that. But—I'm hungry, too. So…

This is an olive branch that becomes a gentle, tentative seduction.

…why don't you—right now—let me…apologize…and maybe…make a little something. For you. For dinner. So that…you don't have to go out for it.

Little beat.

MARK. I don't know, Kelly—

KELLY. Please. Mark. I made a mistake. It was a mistake. Please: Let me try to make this up to you.

Little beat.

MARK. All right.

Little beat.

Then, reciprocating the seduction.

And maybe…I could…make a little something for you, too.

KELLY. That'd be nice.

MARK. 'Cause I can make it a whole lot better than whoever made it for you for lunch. At the luncheon. I know I can.

KELLY. Okay.

MARK. 'Cause dinner is a waaaaay better meal than lunch.

KELLY. Waaaaay better.

Mark goes to kiss Kelly.

As he does so, Kelly shrinks/pulls away from him and turns away, making a face.

[Note: These "shrinks" and "faces" are kind of like what you do when someone smells bad. Big enough to read; small enough to be real. Tip: It's a two-part move. Shrink/pull away first, and then turn away, making a face.]

MARK. Hey! Honey?!?

KELLY. What?

MARK. You just did it again!

KELLY. What?

MARK. You shrank!

KELLY. Oh—

MARK. Away from me! And you made a face!

KELLY. *(Sincerely.)* Oh, no! I'm sorry! I'm so sorry, honey!
> *An awful beat.*
> *Then, Kelly goes in for a conciliatory touch or hug or kiss.*
> *As she does so, Mark shrinks/pulls away from Kelly and then turns away, making a face.*

Honey!

MARK. What?

KELLY. You just did it, too!

MARK. Huh?

KELLY. You shrank! // Away from me! >

MARK. Oh, no!

KELLY. And you made a face!

MARK. I did, didn't I?

KELLY. Yeah, you did!

MARK. I've been doing that, haven't I?!? >

KELLY. Yeah—why?!?

MARK. Oh, no—Kelly:

KELLY. What?

MARK. Remember—… *(A difficult confession.)* Do you remember a few weeks ago when I told you I had a Cobb salad for lunch at that luncheon I had?

KELLY. Yeah.

MARK. I didn't have a Cobb salad.

KELLY. Didn't sound like you.

MARK. I had sex.
> *Little beat.*

KELLY. *(Devastated.)* Oh.

MARK. And I swear to you: It was nothing. It was just what they had. And I was really hungry.

KELLY. Okay.

> *Little beat.*

Um… Do I [know who with]—? Who with?

MARK. Oh, honey, I don't even know.

> *Beat.*

I'm really sorry.

> *Little beat.*

KELLY. Me, too.

> *Long beat.*

I knew, you know. I knew.

> *Beat.*

> *Mark and Kelly are at a complete loss.*

MARK. *(Getting up, resigned.)* Well…I guess I'm [gonna get started on dinner]—…Want me to get started on dinner?

> *Mark starts to go.*

KELLY. No—

MARK. I got pork chops on my way home, there was a special at the SuperCenter.

KELLY. You don't have to make anything.

MARK. Yeah, I do, it's // dinnertime, >

KELLY. No, you don't—

MARK. and it's my turn to cook. >

KELLY. Yeah, but—

MARK. Unless you wanna order in.

KELLY. No—I don't wanna order in, and I don't want pork chops.

MARK. Well, we gotta eat, it's dinnertime.

KELLY. Yeah, well, I'm not really very hungry right now. // I've kinda— >

MARK. Yeah [me neither]—

KELLY. I've kinda lost my appetite.

MARK. Me, too…

Beat.

They're stuck.

Mark sits next to Kelly on the bed.

Of course, you know…if we don't eat…we'll starve.

KELLY. We will.

Long beat.

Then, without looking at each other, Kelly and Mark suddenly reach for each other in the space between them and grab hands at the same exact moment…and hold on for dear life.

Lights slowly fade.

Existential space vacuum sound/music/transition.

And we move on to…

Scene 7: Forgot

It's 7:30 on the same Friday night in the same alternate suburban reality.

Lights up on JILL and KEVIN in the DINING ROOM.

They are sitting at the dining room table eating dessert: Jill's birthday cake.

The cake is covered with a LOT of blown-out candles. (Before it was cut, there were at least thirty-five candles on it.)

Kevin is eating his slice of cake.

Jill is just staring at hers—and at all those candles on the rest of the cake.

KEVIN. Oh, wow! That is so [good]—wow!—I love the whipped buttercream!

Kevin eats some cake.

Mmm! Mm! It's so much better, right?

Jill is not listening.

She is in a daze, preoccupied with the cake.

Sweetheart?

JILL. (*Snapping out of her daze.*) Hm? (*Then, with a smile.*) Oh, yeah—mm—delicious!

KEVIN. You were so right: The regular buttercream just overwhelms the cake, but the *whipped* buttercream…

Kevin takes another bite of cake.

Mm! So good! Good call!

Kevin notices that Jill hasn't eaten her cake.

Jill, you haven't even tried it, sweetheart.

JILL. Yeah—sorry—I'm just—…

Jill starts to laugh.

KEVIN. What? W//hat's [so funny]—?

JILL. That's just…a lot of candles, huh? On my cake?

Jill laughs harder.

Her laughter is strange.

KEVIN. Oh. I guess, yeah.

Kevin laughs, too.

I mean, we're not gettin' any younger!

Kevin and Jill laugh harder.

JILL. Nope! Nope! We're not!

Jill laughs even harder—and maybe a little maniacally.

KEVIN. Are you okay?

JILL. Yeah, yeah. They [the candles] just…

Jill's laughter subsides.

…got me thinkin'…

KEVIN. About what?

JILL. *(Not angry; honestly asking the question.)* Whatever happened to that baby we said we wanted so much?

KEVIN. *(Receives and processes.)* Huh?

JILL. *(Honestly and truly wondering.)* Whatever happened to that baby we said we wanted so much?

KEVIN. *(At a loss.)* Um…

JILL. I only ask 'cause I saw Lori and the girls today. They had a little birthday lunch for me.

KEVIN. Oh, that's nice!

JILL. Yeah, and Lori brought Sophie with her.

KEVIN. Oh!, // Aw!

JILL. Yeah, she's seven months old now!

KEVIN. Get out!, // Wow!

JILL. Yeah, and—anyway—we just got to talking…and Lori asked me…what about us.

KEVIN. *(Receives and processes.)* What about us?

JILL. *(Simply stating a fact and not blaming Kevin.)* She asked me if we were ever gonna have that baby we said we wanted so much.

KEVIN. Uh-huh.

JILL. Yeah, and I said I didn't know., That we were talkin' about it—

KEVIN. Oh?

JILL. Or at least thinkin' about it.

KEVIN. Oh—

JILL. *(Again, simply stating a fact and not blaming Kevin.)* Yeah, and she said that we'd better stop talkin' about it and thinkin' about it… and *do* something about it soon because…the window is closing.

KEVIN. *(Not understanding.)* What…window?

JILL. *(Urgent—but not mean.)* Of opportunity. It's closing. For me. Because I'm not young anymore. I mean, I'm not old, but I'm not young anymore. And…I don't quite know *how* that happened or *when* that happened, but somewhere along the way…we forgot to have the baby.

KEVIN. *(Receives and processes.)* What?

JILL. We forgot to have the baby, Kevin.

KEVIN. What do you mean we forgot to have the baby?

JILL. Here, look.

    Jill offers Kevin her phone.

Read this.

    Kevin reads from the calendar function on Jill's phone.

KEVIN. Friday, September 27th: Meeting with Marie in marketing.

JILL. Yup. Went great.

KEVIN. *(Looking at the phone but responding to Jill.)* Good.

JILL. Keep reading.

KEVIN. Lunch with Lori and the girls. >

JILL. Mm-hm.

KEVIN. SuperCenter.

JILL. Yup—we were out of a couple of things—and…

    Jill points out a specific event.

…what's it say right there?

    Kevin reads.

KEVIN. "Have the baby."

>*Kevin thinks.*

>*And then looks at Jill.*

Have the baby?

JILL. *(Not blaming Kevin—just stating a fact.)* Yeah. I didn't do that today. I did all that other stuff. But not that.

KEVIN. Sweet//heart—

JILL. Today was our target date.

KEVIN. Our what?

JILL. Our target date. For having the baby. We picked it a few years ago, remember?, And I put it in my calendar.

KEVIN. I don't remember picking an actual *day*.

JILL. *(Here's where some pain and, eventually, some rage start to surface.)* Well, *I* do. We said that by the time I was of a certain age would be a good time to have a baby. >

KEVIN. I don't remember us saying that. >

JILL. And I'm of a certain age *now*, Kevin! >

KEVIN. I thought that was just a general kind of "Wouldn't it be nice *if…*" >

JILL. I am a woman of a certain age *today*, Kevin! >

KEVIN. kind of thing, I didn't know you had picked an actual *day*!

JILL. *(Topping him.)* I mean, I woke up this morning and checked my phone to see what I had to do today, and BAM!, There it was!, "Have the baby."

>*Beat.*

>*Then, violently to her phone:*

That's why I *HATE* these things! Everything's too *SMALL*! And you can only see the day you're *IN*! *PIECES* of it! You can't see what's *COMING*! And how are you supposed to *PLAN* and live your *LIFE* when you can't see what's *COMING*?!?

>*Jill slams her phone on the table.*

ARGH!!!

Beat.

Kevin is at a loss.

Finally—trying to be helpful—he gently says:

KEVIN. Sweetheart, there's an alert function. You could have set an a//lert—

JILL. *(Cruelly.) KEVIN!*

Little beat.

Then, kindly:

I'm sorry [I just yelled at you], but—…how did we let this happen? How did we forget to have the baby?

KEVIN. *(Receives and processes.)* Jill: I don't think we forgot to have the baby. We've just been…*busy*, I think. I mean, we've been so busy lately.

JILL. Yeah, I guess. But…doing what? What have we been so busy doing that we forgot to have the baby?

KEVIN. Well—I think we've just been busy getting stuff in order so we *can* have the baby.

JILL. What stuff?

KEVIN. Well, I don't know—do you want some coffee?—

JILL. No—what stuff have we been getting in order?

KEVIN. Just, you know, I thought we wanted to get all our ducks in a row before // we [have a kid]—

JILL. Our *ducks*?!? >

KEVIN. Yeah.

JILL. We don't have any *ducks*, Kevin!

KEVIN. I know [I just]—

JILL. What are you talking about?!?

KEVIN. Well, I don't know, exactly. I just I thought that there were some places we wanted to go and some things we wanted to do— unencumbered—b//efore we—

JILL. *(Not mean—this is a real observation and then a real question.)* We've had *nine* years, Kevin. To go places and do things. Unencumbered. And in nine years, where have we gone?

KEVIN. Lots of pl//aces.

JILL. And what have we done?

KEVIN. Lots of things! We've got a good life, Jill.

>> *Little beat.*

I'm happy. And I thought you were happy. And I thought *we* were happy, just us.

JILL. We are! I just think we could be happier: I want a baby, Kevin. >

KEVIN. Sweetheart—

JILL. Do you?

>> *Little beat.*

KEVIN. Can we talk about this later? >

JILL. No!

KEVIN. Why don't you just eat your cake, and let's // talk about this later.

JILL. Kevin, I don't want to eat my *cake*!

KEVIN. Why not?, I // made it for you!

JILL. Because…that *cake*…is a pretty big part of the reason why I feel like the window is closing!

KEVIN. Wha—why?

JILL. All those *candles*, Kevin!

KEVIN. Huh?

JILL. *(An attack.)* Why would you put that many candles on my birthday cake?!?

KEVIN. Well, because that's how old you are.

JILL. Yeah! Why would you remind me of that?!?

KEVIN. I'm not reminding y//ou [of anything]—

JILL. Why would you remind a woman of a certain age how old she is?!?

KEVIN. Sweetheart—I just thought they'd be pretty!

JILL. Well, they aren't pretty! They're ugly! >

KEVIN. Jill!

JILL. Because they look like what Lori said: that the window is closing!

KEVIN. Jill: Why do you keep saying that?!

JILL. Because it's closing, Kevin!, It's closing!

KEVIN. *(Trying to be helpful.)* Well, you know what they say: Another one'll open!, Another one'll open!

JILL. *(Shutting Kevin down harshly.)* That's *doors*, Kevin, that's *doors*!

> *Little beat.*

KEVIN. [That was unnecessarily mean.] You know what I meant.

JILL. I'm sorry [for being so harsh just now]. I'm sorry. I just—… I thought we wanted a family.

KEVIN. We did. But I just thought that *this*—you and me [without kids]—is what we wanted now.

JILL. No! I think we *forgot* what we wanted!

KEVIN. I thought we forgot on purpose.

JILL. No! I didn't! I had it planned! I've been planning on it!

KEVIN. Well, I haven't been.

> *Little beat.*

I like our life, Jill, // and—

JILL. But don't you think it could be better?

KEVIN. No.

> *Little beat.*

I don't.

> *Little beat.*

I don't want to have a baby, Jill.

JILL. *(Receives and processes.)* Oh.

> *Little beat.*

Okay.

> *Little beat.*

Okay.

> *Jill is crushed.*

Beat.
Then, Kevin defeatedly starts to clear the dishes.
Birthday party's over.
He exits into the kitchen as the lights fade on Jill.
Existential space vacuum sound/music/transition.
And we move on to…

Scene 8: Sick of This

It's 7:30 on the same Friday night in the same alternate suburban reality.

Lights up on ABBIE in the GARAGE sitting on a bench. The bench is next to the door—and it's the place where everyone takes their shoes off before they go inside.

Abbie is in a daze.

A stuffed animal, Dolly Bear, sits at her feet.

Liz enters the garage through the door.

LIZ. Abbie?! Tess came into my office—I told you I was on a call—and said—…

Liz doesn't see Abbie immediately—but quickly finds her sitting on the bench.

Oh—hey—Tess said you were out here looking for Dolly Bear—

Liz realizes that Abbie is in her own world and is not listening to her.

Abs?

ABBIE. Huh?

LIZ. What are you doing?

ABBIE. *(Getting up, producing Dolly Bear, who has been unseen by Liz until now.)* Oh—just—I was looking for // Dolly Bear—

LIZ. *(Seeing Dolly Bear.)* Oh! You found her!, // Thanks!

Liz goes to Abbie and grabs Dolly Bear and heads back to the open door.

ABBIE. Yeah—Tess left her in the car after her playdate with Ellie // today.

LIZ. *(Calling inside the house to Tess.)* Mommie found Dolly Bear, Tess! *(To Abbie.)* Hey, so Caleb [wants to watch *Strike Force Pandas*]—

Abbie sits down on the bench again. She's not herself.

What are you doing?. // Come on!

ABBIE. I just need a second.

LIZ. Well—I've gotta hop back on my call, so could y//ou—?

ABBIE. Just give me a second, Liz.

LIZ. Well—

ABBIE. I'll be right in—just—I need to take a breath.

LIZ. Okay.

> *Liz starts to go inside; stops.*

I'm sorry, but before you take your breath, could you just let Tess know you're still here?

ABBIE. What?

LIZ. Tell Tess you're still here, please.

ABBIE. What?

LIZ. She thinks you're gone again.

ABBIE. What?!?

LIZ. She came up and found me—I was on a *call*, Abbie, I told you, I had a [very important] *call*—and she said she was scared that you were gone again.

ABBIE. What?!?

LIZ. She came and told me that you had gone out to the garage to look for Dolly Bear in the car—but she wanted me to make sure you weren't gone, >

ABBIE. What?

LIZ. so could you just tell her—*show* her—that you're not gone?

ABBIE. Why would she think I was gone?

LIZ. Because you've been out here for a long time, she said, and… you have been kind of not around for us—a lot—lately.

ABBIE. "Kind of not around for you a lot lately?" // What [are you talking about]?!?

LIZ. You've been kind of disappearing on us lately.

ABBIE. Disappearing?!? >

LIZ. Yeah—

ABBIE. What do you mean "disappearing"?!?

LIZ. Well, last weekend, at the SuperCenter, we couldn't find you for twenty minutes.

ABBIE. There was a sale on tires, I was talking with the tire people.

LIZ. And then at the museum?

ABBIE. I had to go to the bathroom.

LIZ. The whole time we were making slime?!?

ABBIE. I don't like sli//me.

LIZ. And then apple picking?

ABBIE. I wanted some cider.

LIZ. So did we all!

> *Little beat.*

I mean—it's all good—she's fine—she was just scared you were gone—really gone, this time—so tell her you're not gone, please.

> *Liz motions for Abbie to go inside and tell Tess she's not gone.*
>
> *Abbie goes to the open doorway and calls to Tess.*

ABBIE. Tess! Mommie's right here!, // Mommie didn't go anywhere!

LIZ. Don't yell to her—go to her and tell her!

> *Liz watches Abbie make her way back to the bench and sit down.*

Abs, what are you doing?, I really have to get back on this call, // and the kids [need you]—

ABBIE. I'll be right in—just give me a second.

> *Little beat.*

LIZ. Okay.

> *Liz starts to go inside again; stops.*

Oh—so, they get to pick what they want to watch for TV time, right, on Friday nights, right?

ABBIE. Yup.

LIZ. Yeah, and well, *Strike Force Pandas* is available on SuperCenter Prime, >

ABBIE. No.

LIZ. and Caleb asked me if // he could watch it—

ABBIE. No—it's too violent, I told him.

LIZ. I know, but his friends are all watching it—

ABBIE. It's too violent, Liz.

LIZ. It's a cartoon for kids!

ABBIE. It's too violent, okay?!?

> *Little beat.*

LIZ. Okay.

> *Liz starts to go inside; stops.*

Are you okay?

ABBIE. Yeah.

LIZ. Okay…

> *Liz starts to go inside again.*
>
> *Abbie spirals into despair and stops Liz with:*

ABBIE. Oh, Liz: No. I'm not [okay]: I was gonna leave.

LIZ. Huh?

ABBIE. Tess was right to have you come make sure I wasn't gone—really gone—because…I was gonna leave. Really leave.

LIZ. What? *(Calling inside through the open doorway.)* Caleb! Watch *Tina Tadpole Goes to Copenhagen* with your sister for Mommie and Mom, and we'll be right there! *(Closing the door and fully engaging with Abbie.)* What do you mean you were gonna // leave?

ABBIE. I came out here and got in the car to look for Dolly Bear… and it was just…so *quiet*. No Tess. No Caleb. So. *Quiet*. And…I just laid down—I was in the back seat—for a second—in all the quiet… and then I saw Dolly Bear under the passenger seat, and I grabbed her and got up and got out of the car, and I was gonna bring her to Tess…but then…I just got back in the car—in the driver's seat this time—and I closed the door—it was so *quiet*—and…I almost started the car and drove away.

I mean—I *didn't* [start the car and drive away]. Obviously. [Because I'm still here.]

But I was going to…because—…

(Getting upset.) Oh, Liz…

LIZ. What?

ABBIE. I'm just…sick of this.

LIZ. Sick of what?

ABBIE. Just…of…a lot of things.

LIZ. Of what things?

ABBIE. Just—…of things like…of you not being home for dinner again tonight!

LIZ. Okay—Abbie, I'm sorry, but I told you, I had a ton to catch up on at work—I c//alled you and told you—

ABBIE. I know, but tonight was a special dinner!, I mean, Caleb got Second Grade Citizen of the Week, and Tess got a Good Sharing Badge, >

LIZ. I know—I'm sorry—

ABBIE. and we had to celebrate without you, and they were so sad about that! >

LIZ. I couldn't get away—

ABBIE. And then—when you finally get home—you have a *call*!

LIZ. I'm sorry—I've just been so slammed lately.

ABBIE. I know. You're slammed. You're always slammed. But I am, too, you know!, >

LIZ. I know—

ABBIE. But you get a chance—when I was in the car all by myself for a second, I realized that you get a chance to…*recover* when you're slammed, because you get time to yourself—so much time to yourself—in your *car*!

LIZ. Huh?

ABBIE. You get to get in your car and drive to work *by yourself* in the morning, and then you get to drive home—after work—in your car—*by yourself*! Do you know what I would *give* to go *any-where* in my *car by myself*?!?

LIZ. *(Starting to comprehend.)* Oh, // Abs, okay [I hear you]—

ABBIE. *And* you have an *office* that you can go to and close the door to and sit in *by yourself*!

LIZ. Okay, // okay—

ABBIE. And you have your office *here*, at *home*, where you can go be by yourself when you're slammed! >

LIZ. I know—

ABBIE. And I don't have any place where I can go be by myself when I'm slammed! And I don't get any time to myself! Ever! And—when I was in the car, all by myself, looking for Dolly Bear— I realized that I'm sick of it—of being stuck here, of having no place for myself, no time to myself, >

LIZ. Abs—

ABBIE. of having to do everything around here by myself, >

LIZ. Okay—

ABBIE. of you just never being here!

LIZ. I'm not "never here," so let's dial down // the histrionics—

ABBIE. Well, you keep not making it home for dinner, and you don't make it home for bedtime half the time, and you watch soccer all weekend every weekend, and >

LIZ. I don't watch soccer all weekend every weekend!

ABBIE. I just do *everything* around here, I feel like, and I am just sick of it, of the way we're doing this—of the way we're…being a family—and I don't think I can do it anymore unless some things change.

> *Little beat.*

LIZ. *(Contritely.)* Abbie, I know how hard it is, what you do, // but—

ABBIE. No, you don't, you have no idea.

LIZ. Okay, you're right, I don't, but listen: I don't know how much things can change right now. Because this is the deal we made. This is how we decided to do this. This is how *you* wanted to do this. You wanted to stay home and do *this* job [be the stay-at-home mom] while I did mine, // and if [you don't want to do it this way any-more, well, let's figure that out]—

ABBIE. I know! But you don't even seem to want to *participate* in my job! I can't participate in your job, Liz. But you're supposed to participate in mine. And you're supposed to *want* to participate in mine!

LIZ. I *do* want to participate in yours, but you don't give me a chance to!

ABBIE. What do you mean I don't give you a chance to?

LIZ. Abbie, you don't like the way I do *anything*!

ABBIE. What do you mean I don't like the way // you do anything?

LIZ. As a *mom*!, You don't like the way I do anything as a *mom*! Because you're the mom, really, I guess, not me, I mean, you had them, you nursed them, they're your kids, it feels like, and nothing I do is good enough for them!

ABBIE. That's not true!

LIZ. Abbie: You don't like what I feed them, how I feed them, how I dress them, how I read to them, what I read to them, how I talk to them, what I pick to watch with them!

ABBIE. That's not true!

LIZ. *(Exploding.)* Yes, it is!!!

ABBIE. Well, // maybe if you actually [did some of those things more often, you'd improve]—

LIZ. *(Angry.)* And, you know what?!? I'm sorry you feel like you do everything around here, // but—

ABBIE. I don't *feel* like I do everything around here, I *do* do everything around here!

LIZ. Okay, well, guess who makes it *possible* for you to do everything around here?, Me!

ABBIE. What?!? No-no-no, that's not [what this is about right now]—!

LIZ. You get so mad at me for working late, but I have to work late—and take after-hours *calls*—so that you can *not* work, you know?!?

ABBIE. Excuse me?!? >

LIZ. *(Correcting herself.)* So you can do *this* job, I meant! >

ABBIE. So I can "not work"?!? Did you actually just say that?!?

LIZ. So you can do *this* job!, So you can do *this* job, I meant!

ABBIE. Not what you said!

LIZ. Abbie: I said—*spoke*—wrong—I'm sorry—what I meant to say was…we have what we need—and we can live the way *you* wanted to—because of me and my job! And I *have* to keep it—my job—so we can live this way, so I have to work *hard*! And I am working *so hard*!, >

ABBIE. Oh, don't—

LIZ. What I do is *hard*, you know?

ABBIE. Don't do that, // pull that! >

LIZ. I'm not *doing* anything! I'm just saying—

ABBIE. That's not what this is about! This is about me doing everything around here because you're never here!

LIZ. Well, I'm not here, because I have to go to work so that there *is* a "here" for you to take care of!

ABBIE. I // said don't do that!

LIZ. And, you know, you're the one who's never here, what with your disappearing act, lately!

ABBIE. I'm here *all* the *time*, Liz!

LIZ. Not for me you're not!

> *Everything stops.*

You're never here for me, Abbie!

> *Little beat.*

I mean, it'd be nice, you know, if you slept. In the bed. With me. More than once in a while. But you don't.

ABBIE. Liz: Tess can't sleep without me right now, you k//now that.

LIZ. I know! And I'm not even upset about that, because Tess needs you, Caleb still needs you, and I need you, too, but I know that they need you more right now, so they get you, and I don't right now, and I'm okay with that, because—right now—I think that's just the way it goes.

ABBIE. Yeah, well, I don't like the way it's going very much // right now.

LIZ. Well, tough, 'cause this is how we decided to do this.

ABBIE. Yeah, well, sometimes I hate the way we decided to do this, >

LIZ. *(Starting to go.)* Well, join the club.

ABBIE. because sometimes the way we decided to do this makes me hate you.

> *This stops Liz for a beat.*

LIZ. W//ow. >

ABBIE. Oh, no—Liz—I didn't—

LIZ. You know, sometimes >

ABBIE. I didn't mean that!

LIZ. the way we decided to do this all makes me feel pretty much the same way, so, we'll call it even.

> *Liz starts to go inside.*
>
> *Abbie stops her with:*

ABBIE. I'm sorry! I'm so sorry! Don't go—I'm sorry! I didn't mean that!

> *Beat.*
>
> *Abbie and Liz exist in the mess they've made for a few seconds.*
>
> *Then:*

LIZ. Okay—um…I'm gonna go watch *Tina Tadpole Goes to Copenhagen* with Tess and Caleb, and then I'm gonna let Caleb watch *Strike Force Pandas*—

ABBIE. But—

LIZ. Abbie, he's gonna get to watch *Strike Force Pandas* tonight—whether you like it or not—because he's Second Grade Citizen of the Week—while Tess and I do tubby-time and book-time and bed-time, okay?!?

ABBIE. Okay, but…you have your call.

LIZ. It can wait. I'm gonna get Tess to bed. And I'll get Caleb to bed. And you just…take a second.

(Gently; generously.) Go for a drive or something.

By yourself.

Liz starts to go inside.

ABBIE. I'm sorry.

Liz stops and turns to Abbie.

LIZ. Me, too.

Liz starts to go again.

Abbie stops her with:

ABBIE. I didn't mean [what I said]—. I don't hate it—the way it's going right now. I love it. Just not right this second.

LIZ. I know.

Liz starts to go again.

Abbie stops her again with:

ABBIE. We'll figure this out, right? We'll figure this out.

Still hurt, Liz wants to say, "Yes," but the best she can give Abbie is:

LIZ. People have been figuring this stuff out—or not—for a long time, so…

Little beat.

Liz starts to go again.

Abbie stops her again with:

ABBIE. Dry Tess's hair. All the way. So it doesn't tangle.

LIZ. I will.

Liz starts to go again.

Abbie stops her again with:

ABBIE. And just so you know—we've already watched *Tina Tadpole Goes to Copenhagen*, and we're up to *Tina Tadpole Goes to Istanbul* now.

Liz does not answer and starts to go again.

Abbie stops her again with:

And I really do think that *Strike Force Pandas* is just too viol[ent]—…

Abbie stops herself, because Liz is just looking at Abbie, her point proven.

You can all watch whatever you want.

Liz turns and goes inside.

Little beat.

Maybe Abbie takes out her keys/key fob and clicks her car unlocked as the lights fade.

Existential space vacuum sound/Music/Transition.

And we move on to…

Scene 9: Destiny

It's 7:30 on the same Friday night in the same alternate suburban reality.

Lights up on the SUPERCENTER.

A MAN and a WOMAN are shopping.

The Man pushes a shopping cart full of stuff a newly single guy might be buying for his new condo.

The Woman pushes a shopping cart with some four-packs of wine and some snacks in it.

After a shopping beat, the Man and the Woman bump carts.

MAN and WOMAN. *(In unison.)* Oh! I'm sorry!, I'm so sorry—

> *The Man and the Woman realize that they know each other—and they are extremely surprised to see each other.*

Oh! Emily/Jake! Hi! Hi!!! What the heck are you—?!? Wow!! Hi!!! This is *crazy*!—Yeah!—*Wow*!!!

JAKE. I can't even believe [I'm seeing you here]!—

EMILY. I know! This is // so *crazy*!!!

JAKE. How are you?!?, How // are you?!?

EMILY. Great!—Wow!—What the heck // are you doin' here, >

JAKE. What are you [doin' here]—?!?

EMILY. in the middle of nowhere?

JAKE. Well—um—I live here, now, actually.

EMILY. *(Confused/surprised.)* Oh.

JAKE. Yeah. Work. They shifted the division here, so—

EMILY. Wow. Here?

JAKE. Yeah, I transferred just—Tuesday, actually.

EMILY. Oh. Wow.

JAKE. Yeah, and what about you? What the heck brings you // to—?

EMILY. Oh, I'm—I was on vacation.

JAKE. Wait—what—*here*?!?

EMILY. No!—I had a connecting flight and missed it—delays—so I'm stuck here overnight. They put me up in a hotel.

JAKE. Oh—at the [hotel over]—by the airport—?

EMILY. Yeah, it's nice!

JAKE. Oh. Good!

> *Beat.*

> *Emily and Jake are amazed that they've run into each other. And they find themselves deeply attracted to each other.*

> *Emily snaps them out of their mutual attraction with:*

EMILY. So how are *you*?!? >

JAKE. Good, good!

EMILY. Boy—you look good!

JAKE. Aw, thanks, so do // you!

EMILY. Really good! >

JAKE. Thanks—

EMILY. Have you been working out? >

JAKE. A little, yeah.

EMILY. 'Cause you didn't used to.

JAKE. No, I didn't.

EMILY. I know, and you *shoulda*!

JAKE. Well, I do now!

EMILY. I guess you do!, 'Cause you look good, pal, mm, *wow*!

JAKE. Thanks! And you're not lookin' so bad yourself!

EMILY. Naw—

JAKE. No, seriously: You look amazing. Wow.

EMILY. Thanks…

> *Emily and Jake are hot for each other.*

> *But Jake remembers that Emily is a married woman, and Emily remembers that Jake is a married man.*

JAKE. S//o >

EMILY. Hey, how's Jennifer—?

JAKE. how's Jonathan doin'?

EMILY. Huh?—Oh!—Good! >

> *Emily doesn't want to talk about Jonathan.*

JAKE. Where'd you guys go [on vacation]—?

EMILY. How's Jennifer?, How's Jennifer?

JAKE. Good!,

> *Jake doesn't want to talk about Jennifer.*

Where'd // you guys go on vacation?

EMILY. I'd love to see her—and the *kids*! How do they like it here? >

JAKE. Um—well—

EMILY. Oh—wait—are they *here*?!? >

JAKE. Um—nope, nope. Where [did you guys go on vacation]—?

EMILY. Is this a little family outing to the SuperCenter?!? >

JAKE. Um…nope—

EMILY. Oh, I'd love to see them, meet the kids!, Where are they?!?, They must be so grown-up!

JAKE. Um—yeah—um—they *are* [all grown-up]!, And…they're not here.

EMILY. Oh.

JAKE. They're—um…they're with Jennifer. Um…Jennifer and I are not together anymore.

EMILY. Oh.

JAKE. We're divorced.

EMILY. Oh, Jake! I'm sorry! >

JAKE. Ah, don't be—

EMILY. I didn't know!, I didn't even know!

JAKE. Well, it was pretty recent, so how could you?

EMILY. Well, I'm so sorry.

JAKE. Don't be. It was a long time comin'. So…don't be.

EMILY. All right! I won't be!

> *Emily and Jake laugh too hard at Emily's attempt to be funny. Awkward beat.*

*We see a flash of how hot they are for each other/how lonely
they are.*

*Jake quickly saves them, again remembering that Emily is a
married woman.*

JAKE. So—how's Jonathan? What were you guys doing for your
vacation? Where'd you go?

EMILY. Um…nowhere.

JAKE. What?

EMILY. *We* didn't go anywhere. Um…Jonathan is…not with me. >

JAKE. Oh.

EMILY. Because—argh! He's—um—…

Emily struggles to find the right words.

*And realizes there really are no right or wrong words in this
case and just comes out with it:*

He's dead.

JAKE. What?!?

EMILY. Yeah, Jonathan died.

JAKE. Oh, no!, // Em! >

EMILY. Yeah.

JAKE. I'm sorry, I didn't even know!

EMILY. Well, it just happened—a few weeks ago—so how could
you [have known]? It was awful. Car accident—freakish—awful.

JAKE. Oh. I'm so sorry.

EMILY. Yeah, so…I've been dealing with *that.*

JAKE. Oh, // Em…

EMILY. And I needed to get my head together. Decided to just go
somewhere far away. *(Getting emotional.)* So…I just picked an island
and went.

JAKE. Argh—I'm sorry, Em. // I'm so, so sorry.

EMILY. *(Recovering.)* Yeah. And the worst and weirdest part is…
we were just about to file for divorce.

JAKE. Oh, no.

EMILY. Yeah. And…then he died.

Little beat.

Which was kind of a relief, actually, *(Trying to make a joke.)* because now we don't have to get one [a divorce]!

Emily laughs sheepishly.

JAKE. *(Receives and processes Emily's terrible joke.)* Oh—yeah!

Jake laughs uncomfortably.

EMILY. Yeah!

JAKE. Wow! That's [funny and awful]…!

EMILY. Yeah!

And Jake and Emily are laughing the way two people would laugh at such a strange, morbid—but kind of fortuitous?— thing.

And then there's an awful silence.

And then they try to save themselves from the awful silence.

Any//way—

JAKE. So, what brings you to the SuperCenter?!?

EMILY. Oh—you know? I don't even know. The hotel listed it as an "area attraction," // so…

JAKE. Oh. Really?!?, // The SuperCenter?!? [An area attraction?!?]

EMILY. Yeah!, And I'm just checkin' it out, gettin' myself some wine—I needed some wine—and they have wine here! In these nifty little four-packs!

Emily shows him the four-pack of wine in her shopping cart.

JAKE. Yeah! Nice!

EMILY. Yeah, so—what about you? What are you doing at the SuperCenter on a Friday night? >

JAKE. Oh—

EMILY. *Lame!*

JAKE. Yeah, yeah, [it *is* a little lame, I know, but] um…I'm just gettin' some stuff for the new place., I got a condo—

Emily has checked out Jake's cart and has noticed…

EMILY. Ferret food?

JAKE. Yeah. I've got a ferret now. They're supposed to be great for companionship if you need…companionship.

EMILY. Oh.

> *Jake is sad.*
>
> *Emily is sad for Jake—then saves him from his sadness and says:*

Well, I didn't know you could get ferret food here!

JAKE. Yeah, they have everything here!

EMILY. Yeah, including your ex-husband!—Or your *first* ex-husband!

JAKE. Yeah!, Or your first ex-wife, as the case may be!

EMILY. Yeah!

> *Beat.*
>
> *Emily and Jake laugh until they realize how pathetic they are.*
>
> *And then Jake rescues them from their patheticness.*

JAKE. Man! This is so crazy—seeing you here!

EMILY. Yeah! It's kind of unreal!

JAKE. Um—YEAH! So…you know what? How 'bout—a toast!

EMILY. What?

JAKE. Yeah! I propose a toast! Can I open one of your little wines, there?

> *Jake grabs a couple of wine bottles from Emily's cart.*

EMILY. Huh? Oh—sure.

JAKE. To you.

> *Jake twists open one of the little bottles of wine and offers it to Emily.*

And me.

> *Jake twists open a little bottle of wine for himself.*

And…chance!

> *Emily and Jake clink and drink.*

I mean—what are the *odds*?!? Both of us here, in this town. On a Friday night. At the SuperCenter?!?

EMILY. Yeah!

JAKE. I mean, we met at one of these [SuperCenters] // way back whenever! >

EMILY. *(Enjoying the memory and mocking it all at once.)* Yeah…

JAKE. Singles Night at the SuperCenter, right?

EMILY. Yeah—I can't believe that was actually a thing!

JAKE. Yeah—me neither—and, anyway, now…here we are [at the SuperCenter] again, both single again. I mean, it kinda feels like a sign or somethin', doesn't it?

EMILY. Yeah.

JAKE. *(Mockingly.)* Like maybe there are mysterious forces at work, here.

EMILY. *(Mockingly.)* Yeah, like maybe the universe is trying to tell us something.

JAKE. Yeah. Like that maybe this is…

> *And it's suddenly stone cold dead serious.*

…destiny or something.

EMILY. Yeah.

> *And suddenly Emily and Jake are kissing passionately in the middle of the SuperCenter.*
>
> *They break away from one another and are stunned—and mortified—for a quick beat.*
>
> *Then:*

EMILY and JAKE. Oh, jeez., Oh, jeez.

JAKE. Okay. You know what? I know this might sound crazy…but do you wanna get outta here?, Come over to my place?, And finish what we just started?, // I think it'd be really fun.

EMILY. *(Advancing.)* Yeah, yes, yes, I do.

JAKE. Great.

> *Jake kisses Emily quickly and passionately.*
>
> *Emily pulls away.*

EMILY. Wait—you know what? I think your place might be too far: My hotel's real close.

JAKE. Okay.

> *Emily kisses Jake quickly and passionately.*
>
> *Jake pulls away.*

No—wait—too far., How about my car!, It's right here!, It's an SUV!, It's big!, It's clean—

> *Jake kisses Emily deeply, quickly, and passionately.*
>
> *Emily pulls away.*

EMILY. No—too far: Bathroom!

JAKE. Too far!

> *And Emily and Jake are kissing again...*
>
> *And they're on the floor being extremely inappropriate in the SuperCenter...*
>
> *For a long time...until they come to their senses and realize how ridiculous what they're doing is...how public it is... and how classless it is...and they stop making out—utterly humiliated.*
>
> *After a horrified little beat:*

EMILY and JAKE. *(In unison.)* Um... *(Smaller horrified beat.)* I'm [so sorry]... *(Even smaller horrified beat.)* Argh! I am so sorry!—No!—Me!—*I* am! Argh!

> *Emily and Jake check to see if anyone saw what just happened...and it looks like no one did.*

EMILY. Okay—you know what? I think I'm gonna go.

JAKE. Yeah.

EMILY. Because this is a bad idea.

> *Emily and Jake get closer and closer to each other with each line they speak in this next sequence until the next kiss.*
>
> *They are saying one thing, but their bodies are doing another.*

JAKE. Yeah. Very bad.

EMILY. 'Cause this is just way too soon for me.

JAKE. Yeah, me too.

EMILY. I'm not ready for anything // like this yet.

JAKE. Me neither.

EMILY. And it's also just really desperate >

JAKE. Yeah.

EMILY. and pathetic >

JAKE. Yeah.

EMILY. and needy.

JAKE. Yeah.

EMILY. And really unattractive.

JAKE. Totally unattractive.

> *And Emily and Jake are kissing again—until they come to their senses again and pull away from each other.*

JAKE and EMILY. *(In unison.)* Argh! Stop it!—What *was* that?!—Argh!

EMILY. What is *happening*?, What just *happened*?!? Argh! What… *happened* [to us]?

JAKE. Well—we just kissed. A lot. >

EMILY. No—

JAKE. And almost did a lot more than that in // the SuperCenter.

EMILY. No—Jake! Come on! What happened to *us*? I mean—right now it feels so stupid that…we didn't make it. What happened?

JAKE. Well…we met, and we fell in love…and we got married…and we got divorced. Just like a lotta people do. That's what happened. Nothin' special.

EMILY. Yeah.

> *Little beat.*

Right now it feels like that was a pretty dumb thing we did. I mean—the divorce part. Not the other stuff.

JAKE. Yeah! It was! So let's start over! Come over!

EMILY. [No] Jake—

JAKE. Come on! I'm being impulsive!, You see that? You never thought I was. >

EMILY. You weren't.

JAKE. Isn't that why we didn't work, you said? I wasn't // spontaneous enough, right?

EMILY. No, no: We didn't work because you didn't really want to be with me!

JAKE. What?!? No!

EMILY. Jake: You tried to break up with me so many times in so many weird ways—I mean, a singing telegram?!?

JAKE. Well—

EMILY. And you could hardly hear it the first time I said I loved you!

JAKE. Well, you surprised me! That was just…*fast*!, And I needed to take things slow, I told you!, And, you know, *you're* the one who didn't wanna even get married!

EMILY. I'm sorry—what?!? *I* wanted to! *You're* the one who holed yourself up in the bathroom on our wedding day all strung out on second thoughts!

JAKE. Yeah, but only because you were having second thoughts, too!, And—hey!—I pulled myself together and went through with it [getting married]!

EMILY. Only because I *made* you pull yourself together! *I'm* the one who got us married!

JAKE. Yeah, well, maybe you shouldn't have [gotten us married]! >

EMILY. You think?!?

JAKE. 'Cause it sure wasn't your thing!

> *The following exchange eventually becomes a heated argument, peaking with Jake's line beginning, "Not my fault."*

EMILY. What?

JAKE. Marriage! It *bored* you! I *bored* you, you said!

EMILY. Yeah, well, it wasn't fun! You weren't fun! I wanted more!

JAKE. Yeah, I guess you did, because you went out and *got* more, didn't you?!? [You had an affair!] >

EMILY. Yeah, >

JAKE. Real classy!

EMILY. well, only because you went out and "got more" first! [You had an affair first!]

JAKE. Yeah, because we did not want the same things anymore! >

EMILY. I know!

JAKE. We didn't see eye to eye on some really important stuff!

EMILY. I know! Like—you didn't want kids, and I did!

JAKE. No-no-no! It's not that I didn't want them!, We were just *busy*!

EMILY. Yeah, well, whatever. You just weren't interested in [my wants and needs]—you were just not good for me!

JAKE. No—you weren't good for me! You just started not being around—disappearing—on me!

EMILY. Well, I was sick of you—of us—of what we had!

JAKE. Well, I was sick of you, too, of what we had, too!, But at least I tried to stick it out!

EMILY. I tried, too!

JAKE. No, you didn't! You left! You're the one who left!

 A little beat as Emily processes this truth.

EMILY. Yup. I am.

 Little beat.

JAKE. And I guess I still don't really understand why. [You left. Because I'm still really hurt and confused about our breakup.]

 Little beat.

EMILY. I guess we just weren't [meant to be]…I guess it just wasn't meant to be.

JAKE. *(Laughing sardonically at his earlier reference to destiny.)* Not our destiny, huh?

EMILY. Huh?—Oh, I guess not.

 Little beat.

JAKE. And neither is this.

EMILY. Huh?

JAKE. Running into you like this. I mean, it's flukey. But…it's not destiny. Is it?

EMILY. No.

> *Little beat.*

> *Jake laughs.*

What?

JAKE. I don't know. Just…how come when two people meet and fall in love and it doesn't work out…how come no one ever calls *that* "destiny"?

EMILY. *(Receives and processes.)* I don't know.

JAKE. *(Proclaiming to the world and trying to be funny.)* "Hey everybody! I met this great woman, and we fell in love, and we got married, but it didn't work out, so we got a *divorce*! It's my DESTINYYYY!"

> *They laugh.*

"And then I met another great woman, and we fell in love, and we got married, and we had a couple of *kids*, but it didn't work out either, and we got a divorce, too! It's my DESTINYYYY!"

> *They laugh.*

EMILY. Or!–OR! "Hey everybody, I met this great guy, and we fell in love, and we got married, but it didn't work out, so we got a divorce, and *then* I met this *other* great guy and *we* got married, but *it* wasn't working out, and we were *gonna* get a divorce, but then he *died*, so now we don't have to get one!, It's my DESTINYYYY!, Woohoo!"

> *They laugh.*

"And now I'm all alone…"

JAKE. Yeah. [Me, too.]

> *A beat as Emily and Jake realize that this is all sadder than either of them expected.*

> *Then, Emily wonders:*

EMILY. How come nobody ever calls *that* "destiny," when they're all alone?

JAKE. I don't know…

> *Sad little beat.*

EMILY. *(Saving them from their sadness.)* You know what?

Emily grabs her bottle of wine.

Another toast. To you. And me. Alone. To…making the most of it.

JAKE. Yeah.

They clink and drink.

Yuck—this [wine] is so bad!

EMILY. Awful.

They laugh.

Then, moving on:

All right—well [I'm gonna go]…

Emily prepares to go.

JAKE. Yeah, I // guess…

EMILY. Yeah, I guess I'll see [ya]—

Emily stops herself and realizes something.

Oh!—…

JAKE. What?

EMILY. I was just gonna say, "I'll see ya"…but I don't know when we'll ever see each other again.

This is a weird and sad realization.

JAKE. Yeah.

Little beat.

EMILY and JAKE. *(In unison.)* But if we *do* [see each other again]—…[If we do see each other again,]…what? [I really-really want to know what you think will happen if we do see each other again, so please-please-please-please-please tell me.]

Little beat.

Nothin'. Yeah. Well, you take care. [Why do we keep talking at the same time?] Yeah. You, too.

They start to go, giving each other one last look.

Bye, Em/Jake.

They exit.

As they do, the Man and the Woman from the first scene of the play, "Obesssive Impulsive," make their way onto the stage, just as they did at the beginning of the play.

We are repeating the opening moment of the play—exactly.

Because we're starting all over.

Because we're always starting all over.

The Man and the Woman see each other and GASP.

As they are just about to kiss…BLACKOUT…into music that seems happy—but is actually sad.

The End
(And the beginning, too.)

BONUS/REPLACEMENT SCENE: "CHICKEN"

The world premiere production of LOVE/SICK included a scene called "Chicken"—which did not make it into the Off-Broadway production, because I wanted to make LOVE/SICK an intermission-less play. And I do think LOVE/SICK works best as an intermission-less play.

But—I love this scene! So I am making it available in two versions that can be used depending on the specifics of your production: Option 1 and Option 2.

Please note that the text of the final scene of LOVE/SICK (Scene 9, "Destiny") is affected if you perform "Chicken." Instructions on how to rewrite Scene 9, "Destiny," are included after Option 2 on page 128.

Adding "Chicken" to LOVE/SICK might make an intermission necessary. The intermission should come after Scene 5, "Uh-Oh."

USES OF "CHICKEN" BASED ON PRODUCTION TYPE

Educational Theater Productions may use Option 1:
A few high school theater directors have asked if they could cut Scene 6, "Lunch and Dinner," from LOVE/SICK, because the scene might not be appropriate for young actors. I am all for this cut for high school productions of the play. But I ask that such productions replace the cut scene (Scene 6, "Lunch and Dinner") with Option 1 of "Chicken."

Since high school theater companies are often looking for plays with large casts, Option 1 of "Chicken" can also be used as an *additional* scene—which will make LOVE/SICK a play for twenty actors. If Option 1 of "Chicken" is used as an additional scene, it must follow Scene 6, "Lunch and Dinner."

Community Theater Productions may use Options 1 or 2:
Community theaters may use "Chicken" only as an additional scene, not as a replacement. If you decide to include it in your production, it must follow Scene 6, "Lunch and Dinner."

Bonus Scene Option 2 is an alternate version of "Chicken" that should only be used in community theater productions where the actors in "Chicken" are beyond child-bearing age.

Professional Theater Productions may use Option 1:

Professional theater companies may use "Chicken" only as an additional scene, not as a replacement. If used as an additional scene, it must follow Scene 6, "Lunch and Dinner."

Professional theater companies may only use Option 1 of "Chicken."

Bonus Scene: Chicken (Option 1)

> *It's 7:30 on the same Friday night in the same alternate suburban reality.*
>
> *Lights up on MADDIE in the KITCHEN.*
>
> *She is pouring sparkling cider into a couple of champagne flutes.*
>
> *She is beaming.*
>
> *After a beat:*

JASON. *(From off.)* Maddie!!!

MADDIE. *(Calling off.)* I'm in the kitchen!

> *After a beat, JASON enters.*
>
> *He's experiencing some inner turmoil.*

Listen, honey: Before we go out, *(Turning to her husband and offering him a flute of sparkling cider.)* I just…I have some news!—

JASON. Maddie, I want a divorce.

> *A little beat as Maddie receives and processes what she has just heard.*

MADDIE. What?

JASON. I want a divorce.

> *Another little beat as Maddie receives and processes what she has just heard.*

MADDIE. Jason… [You're joking, right?] What?

JASON. I want a divorce.

MADDIE. I heard you.

> *Beat.*

Okay. [You're not joking, are you?] What's—…? Sweetie, *why*?

JASON. Because I was just thinking.

MADDIE. About what?

JASON. About getting a divorce.

MADDIE. What? What're y—? Are you serious?

JASON. Yeah.

MADDIE. Okay. Okay.

> *Little beat.*
>
> *Maddie tries her best to make sense of what she's hearing.*

Is there…someone else?

JASON. No! No!

MADDIE. Do you…not love me anymore?

JASON. Yes—no—I mean—I *do* [love you]!

MADDIE. Well then why do you want a divorce?, I don't!

JASON. Because it doesn't feel like it used to.

MADDIE. *(Not comprehending.)* What?

JASON. It doesn't feel like it used to.

MADDIE. What doesn't?

JASON. *It* doesn't.

MADDIE. "It" what?

JASON. It. Us. You and me. >

MADDIE. Jason, I [have no idea what you're talking about.]—

JASON. And I was thinking…that I want it to feel like it felt before, at the beginning.

MADDIE. The beginning of what?

JASON. The beginning of you and me!

MADDIE. Huh?

JASON. I want it to feel like it felt when I first saw you and you first saw me, >

MADDIE. Sweetie [what are you talking about?]—

JASON. the very first time we saw each other!, Do you remember that?!

MADDIE. Yeah.

JASON. It was good!

MADDIE. Yeah!

JASON. So good!

MADDIE. Yeah!

JASON. And true!

MADDIE. Yeah!

JASON. It was beautiful!

MADDIE. Jason—

JASON. And then…

MADDIE. What?

JASON. …it just wasn't. And I want it to be good and true and beautiful again—like it was when I first saw you and you first saw me!

MADDIE. I don't understand—

JASON. Like it was right before we met!

MADDIE. Sweetie—

JASON. Argh, I wish we hadn't done that!!

MADDIE. What?

JASON. *Met*!!!

MADDIE. What? *Met*?!?, // You wish we hadn't *met*?!?

JASON. Well—I wish you hadn't *introduced* yourself to me! >

MADDIE. What're you [talking about]—?!?

JASON. Why did you *do* that?!?, Do you remember doing that?!?

MADDIE. What?

JASON. *Introducing* yourself to me!

MADDIE. Yeah.

JASON. It was a Friday night just like this one and we were standing in line at the SuperCenter just staring at each other, just standing there staring at each other. I couldn't stop staring at you!

MADDIE. Yeah, and I couldn't stop staring at *you*!

JASON. *(Angry.)* Yeah! And everything was perfect, and then *you* just had to walk over to me and say—it was the first time we had ever seen each other—and you *walked* over to me and said, "Hello, I'm Maddie."

MADDIE. *(Receives and processes.)* Yeah.

JASON. *(Accusatory.)* Why did you *do* that?!?

MADDIE. *(Struggling to comprehend.)* Say, "Hello, I'm Maddie," to you?

JASON. Yeah!

MADDIE. Well—it's what people do, Jason, >

JASON. But—

MADDIE. they introduce themselves!

JASON. But you first seeing *me*, me first seeing *you*: That was so beautiful! Why did you have to *ruin* it // by saying, "Hello, I'm Maddie?" >

MADDIE. I didn't know I had *ruined* anything—

JASON. Why did you do that, huh?!?

MADDIE. Well, I guess…

> *Maddie is utterly exasperated…but trying to make sense of this all…which leads her to a pretty great discovery.*

I guess I wanted to know who *you* were, and I wanted you to know who *I* was. And I wanted to see what *we*…could *be*!

JASON. *(Fiercely—maybe cruelly.)* Yeah—and look at what we *are*!

> *Little beat.*

MADDIE. What are we?

JASON. *(Disgusted.)* We're *married*!!!

MADDIE. Yeah! We are! Happily, I thought!

JASON. Well, we *are* [happily married], but…but being happily married—it's not all I thought it was gonna be!, And I miss it—what it *was*, what we *were*, *before* we met, *before* we got married! And that's why I wish you'd never said hello to me, 'cause it was *perfect* before you did that…and it'd all be so perfect still if you hadn't said, "Hello, I'm Maddie"!

> *Little beat.*

MADDIE. If I hadn't said, "Hello, I'm Maddie," to you, Jason, I have a pretty good feeling that we'd have never gotten past just standing there staring at each other. We'd probably still be standing there, staring at each other still.

JASON. Yes: And we'd be happy!

MADDIE. We're not now?

JASON. No! We're angry and settled and frustrated and tense!

MADDIE. Aren't we a little happy in there too?

JASON. Well, yeah—but it's so—argh! It makes me tired!

MADDIE. What does?

JASON. All those things together: the happy, the angry, the settled, the frustrated, the tense! It was simpler before.

MADDIE. Before what?

JASON. Before you said, "Hello, I'm Maddie," because I was lonely! I was only lonely before I saw you! All I did was *long*!

MADDIE. *(Receives and processes.) Long*?

JASON. Yeah! All I did was hope and pray I'd find someone like you, and then I found *you*! Not someone *like* you! But—*you*! Thank God! I don't know what I'd do without you!

> *Jason hugs Maddie hard.*
>
> *Maddie doesn't hug Jason back.*
>
> *Beat.*

MADDIE. *(Removing herself from Jason's hug.)* Jason: If we get a divorce, I'm afraid you're gonna be lonely again. Have you thought about that?

JASON. Yes.

MADDIE. And you're telling me that you'd rather be lonely than be with me.

JASON. Yes. It's simpler to be lonely.

MADDIE. Really.

JASON. Yeah! It's just one thing! I don't want to deal with all that other stuff—the up and down of the happy, the angry, the happy, the settled, the happy, the tense, the happy, the frustrated—that I feel with you. I can't handle it.

MADDIE. Uh-huh.

JASON. I can't!

MADDIE. Uh-huh. So you'd prefer to be lonely.

JASON. Yes.

MADDIE. So you want a divorce. >

JASON. Yes.

MADDIE. Because it's simple. >

JASON. Yes!

MADDIE. Because you can't handle all that other stuff—the angry, the tense, // the frustrated—

JASON. Yes!!

MADDIE. That I've brought on because I said, "Hello, I'm Maddie," to you.

JASON. Yes!!!

MADDIE. Uh-huh.

     Beat.

And what brought you to this realization now?

JASON. Well, I told you: I was thinking.

MADDIE. Oh, that's right, yeah.

JASON. Yeah. I had a minute to think, I guess, and I just remembered…what it [our marriage] *was*, what we *were*.

MADDIE. Uh-huh.

JASON. And it's not that now.

MADDIE. Uh-huh.

JASON. We're not that now.

MADDIE. Uh-huh, and so you want a divorce.

JASON. Yeah. Basically.

     Beat.

MADDIE. What a chicken.

JASON. What?

MADDIE. You are such a chicken.

JASON. What?

MADDIE. I didn't know you were such a chicken.

JASON. I'm not a chicken!

MADDIE. Yeah you are. You're chickening out. >

JASON. No!

MADDIE. And you know what?: I don't think I want to *be* with a chicken. I thought you were just weird, maybe a little high-strung, but never a chicken, but you *are* a chicken, so you know what?, I'll make this real easy for you: I'll just leave *you, (Grabbing her bag, maybe.)* 'cause I don't wanna be with a chicken, so that way you won't have to get a divorce, I'll get it for you, okay? >

JASON. Well…

MADDIE. Okay. So, bye.

> *And—in a flash—Maddie exits, slamming the door behind her.*
>
> *And Jason is alone, dealing with his wife's exit, his new situation—and some newfound loneliness.*
>
> *Long beat.*
>
> *Eventually, Jason starts to panic and rushes to the door, opens it, and calls to his wife.*

JASON. Wait!—Maddie!!

> *Maddie returns.*
>
> *Slowly.*

MADDIE. What?

JASON. I just…I just felt really lonely there for a second—oooh—I think I'm starting to feel really lonely again, Maddie, like I used to feel…

MADDIE. Well—

JASON. And—whoa!—that's…not what I want at all.

> *Beat.*

MADDIE. So what are you saying?

> *Beat.*

JASON. I don't know.

> *Little beat.*

MADDIE. Should I stay, or should I go, Jason?

> *Jason doesn't answer.*

Sweetie, I think this is a decision you're gonna have to make.

JASON. Could you just stay here until I make it?

MADDIE. *(Receives and processes.)* I could do that.

JASON. Thanks. You're good.

MADDIE. And you're a chicken. A very big chicken. And you're weird. You're very weird.

JASON. I love you so much.

MADDIE. Uh-huh.

JASON. Jeez, I don't know where all that came from!

MADDIE. You said you were just thinking.

JASON. I was!, I was! I just get scared sometimes…and I start thinkin' things like…

MADDIE. …that you want to get a divorce?

JASON. Yeah!

MADDIE. Well that is sooome thinkin'.

JASON. I know!

MADDIE. Wanting to just throw it all away because it doesn't feel like it used to feel?

JASON. I'm sorry.

MADDIE. I mean, grow up!

JASON. I'm sorry. I just started thinkin'—

MADDIE. You know what? Shh, Jason. Just shut up. Before you get started again.

JASON. All right.

 Beat.

Boy, I love you!

MADDIE. I love you, too. [But not right now. And I wish you'd stop saying that. Because it's not going to make up for what you just pulled.]

 Beat.

 Jason notices the champagne flutes with the sparkling cider.

JASON. What's this? Ch//ampagne?

MADDIE. Sparkling cider.

JASON. What?

MADDIE. It's sparkling cider.

JASON. Why?

> *Maddie produces a pregnancy test and drops it into Jason's cider.*

What the heck is that?

MADDIE. A pregnancy test.

JASON. What?

MADDIE. It's a pregnancy test.

JASON. Why?

MADDIE. Because I'm pregnant.

JASON. Really.

MADDIE. Yeah.

JASON. Oh.

MADDIE. Yeah.

> *Little beat.*

Now it's *never* gonna feel like it used to feel.

> *We leave Maddie and Jason in a pretty precarious place as the lights fade.*
>
> *Maybe there's a hint of joy, because they're going to be parents.*
>
> *But before they become parents—they have some work to do on their marriage, maybe?*
>
> *Existential space vacuum sound/music/transition.*
>
> *And we move on to Scene 7, "Forgot."*

Bonus Scene: Chicken (Option 2)

[Note: This version of "Chicken" is for middle-aged and beyond-middle-aged actors and should only be used in community theater productions.]

It's 7:30 on the same Friday night in the same alternate suburban reality.

Lights up on Maddie in the kitchen.

She is pouring champagne into a couple of champagne flutes.

She is a little sad—but trying to be happy.

After a beat:

JASON. *(From off.)* Maddie!!!

MADDIE. *(Calling off.)* I'm in the kitchen!

    After a beat, JASON enters.

    He's experiencing some inner turmoil.

Listen, honey: Before we go out, *(Turning to her husband and offering him a flute of champagne.)* I just wanted to say—and I'm saying this not because I'm upset: I know you had a busy day, but I did, too, and I love you—and I know you love me, too—but—and it's okay, but—no—actually, it's not okay, r//eally—um—

JASON. Maddie, I want a divorce.

    A little beat as Maddie receives and processes what she has just heard.

MADDIE. What?

JASON. I want a divorce.

    Another little beat as Maddie receives and processes what she has just heard.

MADDIE. Jason… [You're joking, right?] What?

JASON. I want a divorce.

MADDIE. I heard you.

    Beat.

Okay. [You're not joking, are you?] What's—...? Sweetie, *why*?

JASON. Because I was just thinking.

MADDIE. About what?

JASON. About getting a divorce.

MADDIE. What? What're y—? Are you serious?

JASON. Yeah.

MADDIE. Okay. Okay.

> *Little beat.*

> *Maddie tries her best to make sense of what she's hearing.*

Is there...someone else?

JASON. No! No!

MADDIE. Do you...not love me anymore?

JASON. Yes—no—I mean—I *do* [love you]!

MADDIE. Well then why do you want a divorce?, I don't!

JASON. Because it doesn't feel like it used to.

MADDIE. *(Not comprehending.)* What?

JASON. It doesn't feel like it used to.

MADDIE. What doesn't?

JASON. *It* doesn't.

MADDIE. "It" what?

JASON. It. Us. You and me. >

MADDIE. Jason, I [have no idea what you're talking about]—

JASON. And I was thinking...that I want it to feel like it felt before, at the beginning.

MADDIE. The beginning of what?

JASON. The beginning of you and me!

MADDIE. Huh?

JASON. I want it to feel like it felt when I first saw you and you first saw me, >

MADDIE. Sweetie [what are you talking about?]—

JASON. the very first time we saw each other!, Do you remember that?!

MADDIE. Yeah.

JASON. It was good!

MADDIE. Yeah!

JASON. So good!

MADDIE. Yeah!

JASON. And true!

MADDIE. Yeah!

JASON. It was beautiful!

MADDIE. Jason—

JASON. And then…

MADDIE. What?

JASON. …it just wasn't. And I want it to be good and true and beautiful again—like it was when I first saw you and you first saw me!

MADDIE. I don't understand—

JASON. Like it was right before we met!

MADDIE. Sweetie—

JASON. Argh, I wish we hadn't done that!!

MADDIE. What?

JASON. *Met*!!!

MADDIE. What? *Met*?!?, // You wish we hadn't *met*?!?

JASON. Well—I wish you hadn't *introduced* yourself to me! >

MADDIE. What're you [talking about]—?!?

JASON. Why did you *do* that?!?, Do you remember doing that?!?

MADDIE. What?

JASON. *Introducing* yourself to me!

MADDIE. Yeah.

JASON. It was a Friday night just like this one and we were standing in line at the SuperCenter just staring at each other, just standing there staring at each other. I couldn't stop staring at you!

MADDIE. Yeah, and I couldn't stop staring at *you*!

JASON. *(Angry.)* Yeah! And everything was perfect, and then *you* just had to walk over to me and say—it was the first time we had ever seen each other—and you *walked* over to me and said, "Hello, I'm Maddie."

MADDIE. *(Receives and processes.)* Yeah.

JASON. *(Accusatory.)* Why did you *do* that?!?

MADDIE. *(Struggling to comprehend.)* Say, "Hello, I'm Maddie," to you?

JASON. Yeah!

MADDIE. Well—it's what people do, Jason, >

JASON. But—

MADDIE. they introduce themselves!

JASON. But you first seeing *me*, me first seeing *you*: That was so beautiful! Why did you have to *ruin* it // by saying, "Hello, I'm Maddie?" >

MADDIE. I didn't know I had *ruined* anything—

JASON. Why did you do that, huh?!?

MADDIE. Well, I guess…

> *Maddie is utterly exasperated…but trying to make sense of this all…which leads her to a pretty great discovery.*

I guess I wanted to know who *you* were, and I wanted you to know who *I* was. And I wanted to see what *we*…could *be*!

JASON. *(Fiercely—maybe cruelly.)* Yeah—and look at what we *are*!

> *Little beat.*

MADDIE. What are we?

JASON. *(Disgusted.)* We're *married*!!!

MADDIE. Yeah! We are! Happily, I thought!

JASON. Well, we *are* [happily married], but…but being happily married—it's not all I thought it was gonna be!, And I miss it— what it *was*, what we *were*, *before* we met, *before* we got married! And that's why I wish you'd never said hello to me, 'cause it was *perfect* before you did that…and it'd all be so perfect still if you hadn't said, "Hello, I'm Maddie"!

> *Little beat.*

MADDIE. If I hadn't said, "Hello, I'm Maddie," to you, Jason, I have a pretty good feeling that we'd have never gotten past just standing there staring at each other. We'd probably still be standing there, staring at each other still.

JASON. Yes: And we'd be happy!

MADDIE. We're not now?

JASON. No! We're angry and settled and frustrated and tense!

MADDIE. Aren't we a little happy in there too?

JASON. Well, yeah—but it's so—argh! It makes me tired!

MADDIE. What does?

JASON. All those things together: the happy, the angry, the settled, the frustrated, the tense! It was simpler before.

MADDIE. Before what?

JASON. Before you said, "Hello, I'm Maddie," because I was lonely! I was only lonely before I saw you! All I did was *long*!

MADDIE. *(Receives and processes.) Long*?

JASON. Yeah! All I did was hope and pray I'd find someone like you, and then I found *you*! Not someone *like* you! But—*you*! Thank God! I don't know what I'd do without you!

> *Jason hugs Maddie hard.*
>
> *Maddie doesn't hug Jason back.*
>
> *Beat.*

MADDIE. *(Removing herself from Jason's hug.)* Jason: If we get a divorce, I'm afraid you're gonna be lonely again. Have you thought about that?

JASON. Yes.

MADDIE. And you're telling me that you'd rather be lonely than be with me.

JASON. Yes. It's simpler to be lonely.

MADDIE. Really.

JASON. Yeah! It's just one thing! I don't want to deal with all that other stuff—the up and down of the happy, the angry, the happy, the settled, the happy, the tense, the happy, the frustrated—that I feel with you. I can't handle it.

MADDIE. Uh-huh.

JASON. I can't!

MADDIE. Uh-huh. So you'd prefer to be lonely.

JASON. Yes.

MADDIE. So you want a divorce. >

JASON. Yes.

MADDIE. Because it's simple. >

JASON. Yes!

MADDIE. Because you can't handle all that other stuff—the angry, the tense, // the frustrated—

JASON. Yes!!

MADDIE. That I've brought on because I said, "Hello, I'm Maddie," to you.

JASON. Yes!!!

MADDIE. Uh-huh.

> *Beat.*

And what brought you to this realization now?

JASON. Well, I told you: I was thinking.

MADDIE. Oh, that's right, yeah.

JASON. Yeah. I had a minute to think, I guess, and I just remembered…what it [our marriage] *was*, what we *were*.

MADDIE. Uh-huh.

JASON. And it's not that now.

MADDIE. Uh-huh.

JASON. We're not that now.

MADDIE. Uh-huh, and so you want a divorce.

JASON. Yeah. Basically.

> *Beat.*

MADDIE. What a chicken.

JASON. What?

MADDIE. You are such a chicken.

JASON. What?

MADDIE. I didn't know you were such a chicken.

JASON. I'm not a chicken—

MADDIE. Yeah you are. You're chickening out. >

JASON. No!

MADDIE. And you know what?: I don't think I want to *be* with a chicken. I thought you were just weird, maybe a little high-strung, but never a chicken, but you *are* a chicken, so you know what?, I'll make this real easy for you: I'll just leave *you, (Grabbing her bag, maybe.)* 'cause I don't wanna be with a chicken, so that way you won't have to get a divorce, I'll get it for you, okay? >

JASON. Well…

MADDIE. Okay. So, bye.

> *And—in a flash—Maddie exits, slamming the door behind her.*

> *And Jason is alone, dealing with his wife's exit, his new situation—and some newfound loneliness.*

> *Long beat.*

> *Eventually, Jason starts to panic and rushes to the door, opens it, and calls to his wife.*

JASON. Wait!—Maddie!!

> *Maddie returns.*

> *Slowly.*

MADDIE. What?

JASON. I just…I just felt really lonely there for a second—oooh— I think I'm starting to feel really lonely again, Maddie, like I used to feel…

MADDIE. Well—

JASON. And—whoa—that's…not what I want at all.

> *Beat.*

MADDIE. So what are you saying?

> *Beat.*

JASON. I don't know.

> *Little beat.*

MADDIE. Should I stay, or should I go, Jason?

> *Jason doesn't answer.*

Sweetie, I think this is a decision you're gonna have to make.

JASON. Could you just stay here until I make it?

MADDIE. *(Receives and processes.)* I could do that.

JASON. Thanks. You're good.

MADDIE. And you're a chicken. A very big chicken. And you're weird. You're very weird.

JASON. I love you so much.

MADDIE. Uh-huh.

JASON. Jeez, I don't know where all that came from!

MADDIE. You said you were just thinking.

JASON. I was!, I was! I just get scared sometimes…and I start thinkin' things like….

MADDIE. …that you want to get a divorce?

JASON. Yeah!

MADDIE. Well that is sooome thinkin'.

JASON. I know!

MADDIE. Wanting to just throw it all away because it doesn't feel like it used to feel?

JASON. I'm sorry.

MADDIE. I mean, grow up!

JASON. I'm sorry. I just started thinkin'—

MADDIE. You know what? Shh, Jason. Just shut up. Before you get started again.

JASON. All right.

> *Beat.*

Boy, I love you!

MADDIE. I love you, too. [But not right now. And I wish you'd stop saying that. Because it's not going to make up for what you just pulled.]

> *Beat.*

> *Jason notices the champagne.*

JASON. What's this? Cham//pagne?

MADDIE. Champagne, yeah.

JASON. What?

MADDIE. It's champagne.

JASON. Why?

MADDIE. Happy Anniversary, Jason.

JASON. Huh?

MADDIE. Happy Anniversary.

> *Jason takes this in.*

JASON. Oh.

> *Long beat.*

Well…Happy Anniversary to you, too, honey.

MADDIE. Thanks.

> *We leave Maddie and Jason in a pretty precarious place as the lights fade.*

> *Existential space vacuum sound/music/transition.*

> *And we move on to Scene 7, "Forgot."*

TEXT CHANGES TO SCENE 9: "DESTINY"

If you include "Chicken" in your production of LOVE/SICK, you will need to amend the text in the final scene of the play, "Destiny."

If "Chicken" is being used to *replace* Scene 6, "Lunch and Dinner," in an Educational Theater production, amend the text as follows:
Please go to page 103. Find this line:
JAKE. Marriage. It *bored* you. I *bored* you, you said.

Replace the next 10 lines with this text:

    EMILY. Yeah, well, it wasn't fun! You weren't fun! I wanted more! But at least I tried to make it work! You're the one who decided you just wanted out [of our marriage] outta nowhere!

    JAKE. Yeah, 'cause we weren't at all what I dreamed we could be! And, anyway, we just didn't see eye to eye on some really important stuff. >

    EMILY. I know!

    JAKE. We didn't want the same things anymore.

    EMILY. I know! Like—you didn't want kids and I did!

    JAKE. No-no-no! It's not that I didn't want them!, We were just *busy*!

And then the scene continues as originally written.

If "Chicken" is being used as an *additional* scene in LOVE/SICK, amend the text as follows:
Please go to page 103. Find this line:

    JAKE. Marriage. It *bored* you. I *bored* you, you said.

Replace the next 10 lines with this text:

    EMILY. Yeah, well, it wasn't fun! You weren't fun! I wanted more!

    JAKE. Yeah, I guess you did, because you went out and *got* more, didn't you! [You had an affair.] >

    EMILY. Yeah, >

    JAKE. Real classy!

EMILY. well, only because you went out and "got more," first! [You had an affair first!] And you're the one who decided you just wanted out [of our marriage] outta nowhere!

JAKE. Yeah, because we weren't *at all* what I dreamed we'd be! And, anyway, we didn't want the same things anymore. >

EMILY. I know!

JAKE. We didn't see eye to eye on some really important stuff.

EMILY. I know! Like—you didn't want kids and I did!

JAKE. No-no-no! It's not that I didn't want them!, We were just *busy*!

And then the scene continues as originally written.

PROPERTY LIST

Shopping carts
Business/information card
Roll of toilet paper
Earbuds
2 iPads
Water gun that is painted to look like a real handgun. [Note: Realistic-looking water guns are difficult to find. Find realistically *shaped* water guns (they're colorful) and paint them black.]
2 smartphones
Magazine
Birthday cake with at least 35 candles, slices cut out
Stuffed teddy bear
Bottles of twist-top wine, snacks
Items in shopping cart that a newly single guy would be buying for his new condo

SOUND EFFECTS

Existential space vacuum sound/music

NOTES FOR ACTORS AND DIRECTORS

On the play:

LOVE/SICK is not a realistic or naturalistic play, but it should feel like one. Each play in the cycle should be played realistically, naturalistically—until it explodes into the fantastical, the strange, the outrageous. Scene 1, "Obsessive Impulsive," is the exception: It is fantastical and strange and outrageous from the get-go, but—sadly—ends in a more realistic place. But in all of the other plays, the fantastical, strange, and outrageous elements must all emerge undetected. I don't want LOVE/SICK to *feel* strange before it *becomes* strange. So don't telegraph the strangeness. Let it sneak up on people. If you do this, LOVE/SICK will be more surprising for audiences. And this play must be surprising. Always. It must constantly pull the rug out from under the audience. Every reversal in this play should make the audience gasp. What thrills audiences—and what really makes them laugh—is the *surprisingly* strange and surreal places this play takes them.

In developmental productions of LOVE/SICK, I found it helpful to remind directors to tell the actors this: Don't play the end of any of these plays at the beginning. Don't play the known outcome (which is often sadness, despair, utter uncertainty) of any of these plays at the beginning. Fight to solve the problems you're facing before you descend into despair and pain. This will keep the play as a whole surprising and buoyant.

It may help to think this way: Each play in LOVE/SICK (except Scene 1, "Obsessive Impulsive") starts off in a simple, normal place in which one partner is living the status quo and the other partner is in crisis; then each play gets surreal or strange or fantastical or outrageous as we reach a climax; and at the climax, each play bursts into painful, deep, multidimensional truth. Only when each play has burst into that painful, deep, multidimensional truth are you allowed to let in the despair.

Don't get defeated too soon. If you are defeated too soon, LOVE/SICK will be a silly dirge. And LOVE/SICK is not a silly dirge. It's a serious comedy. It's all about tricking audiences, getting them laughing, and then gut-punching them with the depths it probes. If the plays feel tragic too soon, you'll lose the fun and the funny. And I want LOVE/SICK to be fun and funny. Until it's not. I want to make people wonder, "I was just laughing hysterically. How the heck did we get to this awful place?!?"

Finally, make audiences feel the *love*…and then the *sick*. The play is called LOVE/SICK, after all. The people in this play love each other desperately. And they're all a little sick. (They are human beings, after all.)

And, yes, LOVE/SICK is a comedy—but it is filled with despair. Don't skip the comedy. Don't cheat the despair.

On the characters:

Remember—the characters in LOVE/SICK aren't quirky. They're pretty ordinary people dealing with extraordinary circumstances. It's the *circumstances* that are quirky.

The characters in LOVE/SICK are desperately trying to solve their problems. They remain *positive*—until they just can't anymore.

The characters in LOVE/SICK are always in discovery mode. And when they make a discovery, they are *consumed* by that discovery. Find the discoveries in this play. And play them *fully*. They should be gasp-inducing—literally. Actors who do this play should gasp over and over and over. The discoveries in LOVE/SICK should force inspiration. And inspiration literally means "breathing in." We breathe in new ideas—audibly—in everyday life. Do the same in this play: Gasp.

The characters in LOVE/SICK are quite transparent—and mercurial. When they feel joy, they are as joyful as can be, so that when they crash-land into despair or rage, it is devastating and even terrifying for all of us. When they are sad or angry, they are as sad and as angry as can be, so that when they bounce back to joy, it is a wonderful ride for all of us. Watching them bounce from joy to despair to rage to terror to insanity and back to sanity— usually in an instant—well, that's the ride you need to take (and take audiences *on*) with this play.

The characters in LOVE/SICK don't live ironically. (Irony kills drama.) They don't comment on what's happening to them. They don't editorialize as they live. They are unaware of what's coming at them. And so—they are constantly getting blindsided. And sur- prised—which is actually what happens to us all in real life.

We all try so hard to be in control of our lives, but we get blindsided on a daily basis. Because we just don't know what's coming! When this play was first published, contemporary comedy was heavily dependent on irony and seemed to be convinced that we are in control of what happens to us and that we are all smart enough to be able to comment on our lives while we are living them. I don't think this is true at all. We are not in control. We get smacked down by life all the time. And watching people get smacked down by life is just awful. And heartbreaking. And about as hilarious as it gets. (Smackdowns make for good drama—and good comedy.)

The characters in LOVE/SICK are not (generally) sarcastic. Actors: Use sarcasm sparingly. A good way to accomplish this is to activate the questions the characters in LOVE/SICK ask. *Really ask* the questions. *Really seek* answers. Rarely do the people in this play (or in real life) ask questions sarcastically, rhetorically, or knowingly. They *really* ask the questions because they *really* want answers. Because they really *don't know* the answers.

The characters in LOVE/SICK are not angry. They're hurting. There are angry explosions in every play in LOVE/SICK, but that anger comes from the hurt and the pain that the characters are experiencing. Rarely is this anger solely manifested as an aggressive attack on another person. It is usually manifested as confusion, pain, and desperation. It's a cry for help. Remember—the people in this play are desperately trying to solve their problems. They remain *positive* against all odds. *They solve their problems by enlisting their partners' help, not by pushing them away.* The characters in plays four through nine (and in Bonus Scene Options 1 and 2, "Chicken") are saying, "I am not very happy with you/us right now and I need you to help me figure out how to make me happy with you/us again. Right. Now."

The characters in every scene in LOVE/SICK experience what I like to call "despair swallows" or "despair free falls"—which are feelings of existential despair so intense that they make a person feel like the earth is opening up and swallowing them. There's at least one despair swallow or despair free fall in every play in LOVE/SICK. Find them. And play them fully. They're physical. But not fake.

The characters in LOVE/SICK think physically. Actors: Always let us see you sort through the crazy things that happen to you in this play. It's thrilling to watch people think and figure stuff out, because people actually think with their whole bodies.

The characters in LOVE/SICK are not caricatures. They are real people—feeling HUGE feelings. Actors: Keep them grounded. Play the truth of the moment—all the while remembering how high the stakes are. Feel deeply. And think about this: What would you actually—*actually*—do in each situation? That will keep you honest and true while you execute the theatricality called for in the play.

On the arc of the piece:
Each play in LOVE/SICK can stand alone and should be able to stand alone. However, the plays work together, using many stories to tell one story, and that story is a chronicling of the life cycle of a relationship—kind of an *e pluribus unum* thing. I described this "one story" idea to director Sally Wood like this, and she found it tremendously helpful:

"Obsessive Impulsive" is the meeting part.

"The Singing Telegram" is the breakup part/getting-out-of-a-bad-relationship-so-you-can-open-yourself-up-to-the-possibility-of-actually-finding-some-real-love part.

"What?!?" is the first-time-we-said-I-love-you-to-each-other part.

"The Answer" is the wedding part.

"Uh-Oh" is the being-married-is-a-little-harder-than-I-thought-it-would-be part.

"Lunch and Dinner" is the affair part.

[Bonus Scene] "Chicken" is the married-life-isn't-quite-what-I-thought-it-would-be part.

"Forgot" is the we-don't-want-the-same-things-anymore-so-would-we-be-better-off-if-we-split-up? part.

"Sick of This" is the now-that-we-have-kids-how-do-we-keep-our-marriage-healthy? part.

"Destiny" is the we-tried-and-we-failed-but-we-will-try-again-because-we-have-to-keep-trying-but-not-with-each-other-because-we've-learned-from-our-mistakes part.

On stage directions:
Many of the stage directions in LOVE/SICK are as important as the dialogue. They are actions that are crucial to telling the story. Don't ignore them. They will help you.

NOTES FOR DIRECTORS

On the play:
LOVE/SICK is a tough play to direct. It's nine different plays. You have nine different stories to tell—as part of one story. Tell each one well and the whole will take care of itself.

LOVE/SICK is a cinch to *do*. But it's very difficult to rehearse and put together. Know that actors generally struggle to learn their lines. But once they learn them, the play (I've been told) is really fun—and actually quite easy—to do.

On rehearsing:
If four actors are performing this play, I highly recommend calling all of your actors all of the time. That way the two actors you are not working with can run lines/help each other run lines. This play is tough to learn.

On the kisses in Scene 1, "Obsessive Impulsive":
The kisses in "Obsessive Impulsive" can be dangerous for actors if they try to kiss each other unrehearsed. Lips will get bloodied. Teeth might get chipped. For early rehearsals, I suggest doing the action of the kisses without physical contact—but with the physical intention of kissing and with this sound: "mmmmm." Using this method, actors will learn where the kisses are. Once the play is sculpted and actors are off book, slowly add the actual kisses—and the physicality of the kisses. They need to be choreographed—for safety's sake. But they must seem impulsive!

On transitions:

Be creative. Make them interesting. Don't let the audience rest—but give them time to process what has just happened. I feel like there's a *Twilight Zone* quality to this play—one that could be explored gently in the transitions. I think that's what I'm looking for when I call for an existential space vacuum sound in between each play—something *Twilight Zone*-ish. Many have asked me what this existential space vacuum sound is. I think it's just the sound of the fear of being all alone. In the world. In the universe.

On the music:

Interstitial music will play a big part in LOVE/SICK. Julian Fleisher wrote music for the world premiere of the play, and it is available for licensing through Dramatists Play Service. You can find more information on ordering and licensing this music by going to the LOVE/SICK page on www.dramatists.com. I strongly encourage its use!

NOTES FOR DESIGNERS

On the set:

With the exception of the first and last play, all of the plays in LOVE/SICK take place in different rooms of a house.

LOVE/SICK has been presented on an empty stage with minimal scenic elements and a door that could be moved to different locations; it's been presented with a cutaway view of a home as a backdrop, using minimal scenic elements and a door that could be moved to different locations; it's been presented on a turntable divided into thirds; it's been presented on a set with the SuperCenter as a backdrop, with props and scenic elements pulled from the SuperCenter, and a door that could be moved to different locations. It's also been presented on a set that looked like the blueprint of a home: Scenic elements were built into and popped out of this set, and a movable door was used. (The name of each play was written on the walls with chalk as each play commenced. It was pretty cool.)

I've always wondered how this would work: A compressed cutaway of a suburban home could serve as the backdrop, with furniture and props crammed into each room, and pulled out and used and replaced as necessary.

Note that a door factors into every play except for the first one and the last one.

On costumes:
The people in LOVE/SICK are solidly middle to upper-middle class. They dress decently. Urbanites: Don't condescend.

NOTES FOR ACTORS

On punctuation:
Please review the notes on punctuation and stage directions section on Page 16 of this manuscript.

On language:
The expression "Argh" is meant to be a sound of exasperation. It's not a directive to talk like a pirate. So—make any sound of exasperation you wish when you see "Argh" in the script.

More specific notes on the stage directions:
Many of the stage directions in LOVE/SICK are as important as the dialogue because they are actions that are crucial to telling the story. Don't ignore them. They will help you.

The stage directions are particularly crucial in parts of Scene 1, "Obsessive Impulsive" (in the simultaneous dialogue sequences; in all the kissing sequences; in the advancing and retreating at the end; in the last moment); in Scene 3, "What?!?" (where Andy and Ben do and don't make eye contact; when Andy tries to say, "I love you," to Ben; in the last moment); and in Scene 6, "Lunch and Dinner" (in the shrinking and making faces moments; in the last moment).

I only write this because I have spoken to actors who have crossed out all of the stage directions in the play so they could discover it for themselves—and they've struggled. I'm all for actors discovering stuff—but not when it creates more work than necessary. Crossing out all of the stage directions means you're crossing out crucial parts of the story. Let the stage directions help you. I promise you they will—and they will free you so you can make the play your own.

On playing multiple characters:
If you are playing multiple characters in LOVE/SICK, don't obsess over drastically differentiating the characters. The stories will take care of that. Tell each story, and distinct characterizations will reveal themselves. A tip: The couple in "Obsessive Impulsive" (the first play in the cycle) are the most innocent people in the play. The couple in "Destiny" (the last play in the cycle) are the most world-weary (but not defeated!) people in the play.

On Scene 1, "Obsesive Impulsive":
"Obsessive Impulsive" is a funny play—but remember that the Man and the Woman could get in serious trouble for kissing each other in public. Remember that every apology they make is utterly sincere. Most important: Remember that this is the first time either of these people has ever fallen in love.

A tip on speaking in unison: Break down all unison speeches into dialogue. Rehearse the dialogue, allowing each actor to play both sides of the dialogue. This will help with clarity. Those unison speeches must feel like dialogue so we can hear the story amidst all the ridiculousness. Also, remember that speaking in unison doesn't mean that your eyes must be locked. As you work on the opening speech, experiment with where you are making eye contact and where you aren't. (The dialogue exercise should help with this.)

A reminder about the kisses: The kisses in "Obsessive Impulsive" can be dangerous for actors if they try to kiss each other unrehearsed. They need to be choreographed—for safety's sake. But they must seem impulsive! See page 135 for more info.

On Scene 2, "The Singing Telegram":
The Singing Telegram Man does not want to sing his song to Louise once he realizes how she feels about Greg. He is trepidatious. But— Louise must not see too much of his trepidation or she will seem oblivious to the discomfort the Singing Telegram Man is feeling. Figure out where we can see how unsettled the Singing Telegram Man is—unbeknownst to Louise.

On Scene 5, "Uh-Oh":

Note to the actress playing Sarah: In my mind, this play begins as a test. You have a fairly cruel practical joke to play. And you're not entirely sure you want to play it—but, as the play unfolds, you're forced to play it, because your husband has failed you and has no idea that he has. Because he doesn't contribute to the fun factor in your relationship anymore. You believe that Friday nights and weekends should be for fun. And—for you—the past bunch of Friday nights and weekends have not been fun. They've been a total bore. And you don't want to be bored. So you are taking action—to save your marriage.

If, when you say, "I'm *bored.*" on page 57, Bill were to respond with something like, "Oh, no! Honey! You shouldn't be bored! I'm so sorry! Let's go do something fun!" *that* would solve the problem, and there would be no need for you to execute the prank. But Bill doesn't say anything like that. He says, "Okay. Okay. Okay. Honey: I think I might know what this is. You're just—I think…you know what? This is just what happens." And that is unacceptable—and marks the point of no return. The gun must be pulled—in order for you to wake Bill up and save your marriage.

Bill—and the audience—should have no idea that you are playing a joke. Good pranksters don't give any indication that they're playing a joke. And you should be TOTALLY PUMPED that you succeeded so wildly at pulling off your prank.

On Scene 7, "Forgot":

Note to the actress playing Jill: Jill is not angry at the top of this play. She is coming to a realization. And she is appealing to Kevin to help her process this realization. The anger comes when she loses it because the calendar on her phone has let her down.

On Bonus Scene, "Chicken":

Note to the actors in "Chicken": Jason is experiencing a midlife crisis. He's frustrated and angry, because his life is not what he thought it would be, and he is desperately trying to figure out how to make it what he thought it would (or could) be. Unfortunately, Jason has decided that a divorce is the best way to make his life better. Even though he loves his wife and really doesn't want a divorce. Maddie has seen Jason spiral out of control before. She is familiar with his pouty, childish tantrums. But Jason usually spirals out of control and throws tantrums over things like…not being able to find the remote…or realizing there aren't any more Cheerios. This time, though, he's spiraling out of control over something that is hurting his wife—deeply. Fortunately, Maddie knows how to handle Jason. And, in this scene, she does. Expertly.

Hello, actors, theatre makers, and theatre fans,

On behalf of Broadway Licensing Global and the author(s) of this work, we thank you for your continued support of the arts and the playwrights you love.

Like every title in our catalogue, this play is covered by copyright law, which ensures authors are rewarded for creating new dramatic work and protects them from theft and abuse of their work. We are compelled to impress upon all who obtain this edition that **this text may not be copied, distributed, or publicly produced in any way,** nor uploaded to any file-sharing websites or software—public or private. Any such action has an immediate and negative effect on the livelihood of the writer(s)—it is also stealing and is against the law. As a result, should you copy, distribute, or publicly produce any part of this text without express written consent and licensed permission from our company—even if no one is being paid and/or admission is not being charged—your organization shall be subject to legal consequences that we are sure you want to avoid.

But we have faith in you and your understanding of these guidelines!

While this acting edition is the only approved text for performance, there may be other editions of the play available for sale. It is important to note that our team has worked with the playwright(s) to ensure this published acting edition reflects their desired text for all future productions. If you have purchased a revised edition from us, that is the only edition you may use for performance, unless explicitly stated in writing by our team.

Finally, and this is an important one, **this script cannot be changed in any way** without written permission from our team. That said, feel free to reach out to us. We don't bite, and we are always happy to have a discussion to see if we can accommodate your request.

We are thrilled this play has made it into your hands and we hope you love it as much as we do. Thank you for helping us keep the theatre alive and well, and for supporting playwrights, in our continued journey to make everyone a theatre person!

Sincerely,
Fellow theatre lovers at Broadway Licensing Global

Note on Songs/Recordings, Images, or Other Production Design Elements

Be advised that Broadway Licensing neither holds the rights to nor grants permission to use any songs, recordings, images, or other design elements mentioned in the play. It is the responsibility of the producing theater/organization to obtain permission of the copyright owner(s) for any such use. Additional royalty fees may apply for the right to use copyrighted materials.

For any songs/recordings, images, or other design elements mentioned in the play, works in the public domain may be substituted. It is the producing theater/organization's responsibility to ensure the substituted work is indeed in the public domain. Broadway Licensing cannot advise as to whether or not a song/arrangement/recording, image, or other design element is in the public domain.